Attend the World Cup Like a Pro

The Ultimate Fan Guide, Tips, Tricks, and Tales for Your Supreme World Cup Experience

Paul Prosper

Disclaimer

The information in this book is intended for general purposes only. Paul Prosper provides this information, and while we strive to keep it updated and accurate, we make no representations or warranties of any kind, either express or implied, regarding the completeness, accuracy, reliability, suitability, or availability of this publication or the content, products, services, or related graphics it contains for any purpose. Therefore, any reliance on such information is strictly at your own risk. In no event will we be liable for any loss or damage, including, without limitation, indirect or consequential loss or damage, or any loss or damage whatsoever arising from loss of data or profits arising out of, or in connection with, the use of this publication. Through this publication, you can link to other resources and contacts that are not under the control of Paul Prosper. We have no control over the nature, content, and availability of those responsible for their management, operation, or function. The inclusion of any links does not necessarily imply a recommendation or endorse the views expressed within them. At the time of writing, every effort was made to keep the information in this publication current. However, Paul Prosper takes no responsibility for, and will not be liable for, information being out of date or unavailable due to technical or any other issue beyond our control.

Contact: Paul Prosper - prosperouspublishingco@gmail.com

ISBN: 9798310078277

Attend the World Cup Like a Pro

The Ultimate Fan Guide, Tips, Tricks, and Tales for Your Supreme World Cup Experience

Paul Prosper

Dedicated

This book is dedicated to football lovers, also known as soccer in some countries, and especially to the true, devoted fans who will spend their last yen, euro, dollar, or pound to travel to all corners of the world to watch a game.

Your Free Gift

As a token of my appreciation for your purchase of my book, I am offering my on-page World Cup Guide for free to my readers.

To get instant access, go to:

https://mailchi.mp/pprosperllc/worldcupguide

This guide will be your one-page checklist for important information you will need to attend the World Cup like a pro.

Table of Contents

Acknowledgments

I want to express my deepest gratitude to my family for their unwavering support throughout this journey. To my partner, who endured late nights and countless revisions with a smile, and to my baby boy, who inspired (and interrupted) me with his boundless energy. Thanks to my mother for championing this project from start to finish.

About the Author – Paul Prosper

Globetrotting professor, retired US Air Force veteran, and financial enthusiast Dr. Paul Prosper shares his insights on building wealth, investing wisely, and creating a life filled with purpose and fulfillment.

As an immigrant who traveled from Jamaica to the United States, Paul dedicated 20 years to the Air Force, achieving financial independence while following his passion for worldwide exploration. He particularly focused on experiencing the FIFA World Cup firsthand. Now back in his beautiful homeland of Jamaica, he enjoys sharing his knowledge as a part-time adjunct professor with students, friends, readers, and coaching clients.

His books explore personal finance, investment strategies, self-improvement, and the art of crafting a life rich in experiences and happiness. Join him on a journey of discovery and unlock your potential for an enriching life.

Kickoff

This book aims to help football fans and travelers plan their first World Cup experience. Throughout *Attend the World Cup Like a Pro*, I hope to inspire football fans and world travelers to book the trip of a lifetime and enjoy a future World Cup. I have been fortunate enough to attend every World Cup since 2010 – I attended South Africa in 2010, Brazil in 2014, Russia in 2018, and Qatar in 2022.

In this book, I share the most important lessons I learned so you don't repeat my mistakes while planning for and attending the World Cup. I also share my most memorable stories, thoughts, and tips to help ensure you enjoy your World Cup trip and fully immerse yourself in the experience. Lastly, this book is for world travelers. If you enjoy exploring the world and immersing yourself in foreign cultures and experiences, this book is for you.

If you are interested in attending a World Cup but do not know what to expect, this book offers fresh perspectives to help make your next World Cup an even more memorable experience. If you have hesitated to book the flight and purchase game tickets, this book will help alleviate those fears, and you can enjoy the world's greatest international sporting event while creating unforgettable memories.

In this book, I only reference the Men's World Cup since that's the only World Cup tournament I have attended. I am also a fan of the FIFA Women's World Cup. I planned to attend the 2019 FIFA Women's World Cup in France to support Jamaica's Reggae Girlz. However, duty called, and the United States Air Force ordered a permanent change of station. I had to move from Colorado to Oklahoma that summer. Hopefully, I will be in Brazil cheering for Reggae Girlz in 2027.

The FIFA World Cup has been held every four years since 1930. However, due to World War II, there was no World Cup in 1942 and 1946. 32 teams participate in the World Cup, with the World Cup Final match culminating three years of global FIFA World Cup qualifying. FIFA recognizes over 200 men's national teams, which are reduced to 32 World Cup qualifying teams.

Here's how the World Cup is structured.

- **World Cup Qualification:** This happens during the three years leading up to the World Cup.

- **Group Stage:** The 32 qualified teams are randomly divided into eight groups of four. All teams within a group play each other. This is the only stage where games can end in a tie. Teams earn 3 points for a win, one point for a tie, and zero points for a loss. The two teams in each group with the most points advance to the next round.

- **Round of 16:** 16 teams are paired against each other in a single-game elimination match.

- **Quarterfinals:** The final eight teams play each other in another single-match elimination round.

- **Semifinals:** The final four teams compete in two single elimination matches.

- **Final:** The final two teams play for the most coveted championship trophy in the world.

Winning the World Cup is the essence of being a World Champion. You bracket up in a tournament against the world and win. The 2026 World Cup will feature 48 teams, a first for the World Cup. This means that after the Group Stage, there will be a Round of 32, then a Round of 16. I'm not too excited about this rise in the number of teams. This is because the groups in the group stage may be "watered down." I'm afraid there will no longer be a "Group of Death." The term "Grupo de la Muerte" was coined by Mexican journalists in the 1970 World Cup, referring to Group C, comprised of Brazil, England, Czechoslovakia, and Romania (Motson & Brownlee, 2006). A Group of Death happens when at least three or all four teams in a group are expected to advance, but only two teams can advance to the next round. The chances of a Group of Death happening in a tournament of 48 teams will be slim.

My earliest memory of the World Cup was in 1986. I was six years old, and the tournament was in Mexico. At the time, I lived in Kingston, Jamaica, and I remember that the games seemed to stop the entire island. People gathered to watch games anywhere there was a TV or listened on radios turned up loud for everyone within earshot to hear. Diego Maradona's goal of the century and his notorious "Hand of God" on his way to winning the 1986 World Cup was my official introduction to the FIFA World Cup. The beautiful game had me hooked.

In 1994, the USA hosted the World Cup. I lived in New York, and the host stadiums were nearby: Giants Stadium in New Jersey was the closest. World Cup stadiums were not too far away in Philadelphia and Washington, D.C. However, I was a broke 14-year-old, and I could only enjoy the World Cup by watching the games on TV. I've never been so close to a World Cup as I was during USA 1994.

I later regretted being close to the World Cup but not attending any games or festivities. I should have tried to convince my mom to let me take a train with friends to Giants Stadium to watch the reveling fans and soak up the vibrant atmosphere, even if I had no game ticket. I knew nothing about Fan Zones or viewing parties at the time. One of the reasons I wrote this book is to, hopefully, motivate and inspire anyone who has been in my shoes, wanting to attend the World Cup but unsure of how to make it happen.

France 1998 was another fantastic tournament that I watched on TV. I was a broke college student back then, and summer was my only opportunity to make some money working. This one was extra special to me because it was the first (and only) World Cup Jamaica's Reggae Boyz ever qualified for. I often wonder how nice it would have been to be in a stadium watching my birth nation, Jamaica, play.

Then came Japan/Korea in 2002. I was in training in the Air Force and was not allowed to take leave. I had not yet committed to going to the World Cup. However, the 2006 World Cup in Germany was the first time I seriously considered attending the World Cup in person. My cousins went to Germany during this World Cup and stayed with my oldest brother, who was stationed there. When the USA vs. Italy group stage game in Kaiserslautern was days away, I seriously considered catching a C-17 military flight to Ramstein Air Base in Germany. However, I was not able to do so because of job constraints and insufficient planning time. When I think about it now, I want to kick myself. My brother lived in a World Cup host nation, and I did not take advantage of that.

Looking back, I can relate that experience to many other experiences I have had in life. I didn't know anyone who had done what I wanted to do. I did not know anyone who had attended the World Cup; therefore, I was unsure of how to get there. I knew I had to make it happen. And since I'm not one to gatekeep experiences, I wrote this book so you can access the mind, thoughts, and strategies of someone who figured it out and made it happen. I want to help you avoid being stuck in the "I don't know where to start" rut.

When I discovered that the 2010 World Cup would be in South Africa, a continent and nation I had never been to but had always wanted to visit, I made my decision. It was easy. I was committed. South Africa 2010 would be the first World Cup I would attend; no more excuses.

Getting to Your First World Cup

Nearly a quarter of the world's population tunes in to watch a single sporting event, the World Cup final match on TV. Why? This chapter will explore the global appeal and significance of the World Cup, share my experience attending my first World Cup, and highlight some essential factors to consider when planning your own visit to this event.

The Allure of the World Cup: Understanding the Tournament's Global Appeal and Cultural Significance

How do I explain the global appeal of the World Cup? It is hard to explain when people ask me what going to the World Cup is like. An explanation rarely ever does the experience justice. Kamau (2024) said, "It is more than a football tournament; it is a global celebration of unity, culture, and passion." (para. 1). I feel like the World Cup is the pinnacle of national pride and patriotism. Nowhere have I seen so many happy people from so many different nations in the same place for the same reason, all having a good time with national pride on full display. It is the ultimate opportunity to increase your cultural capital. It's a party with the world centered on football games. Watch games all day and party all night with people from all over the world, then do it again the next day. It is an all-in-one cultural, sporting, travel, and learning experience.

There are so many people at the World Cup—millions of people! The World Cup is such a big event that it takes entire nation(s) to host it, unlike the Olympics, which is hosted by a single city. Seeing so many people unite in peace and unity to celebrate the beautiful football game is a sight to behold. The spectators' emotional connection to the beautiful game makes the World Cup a special tournament. The ups, downs, cheers, and tears make the World Cup an emotional rollercoaster and a cultural showcase.

You can sit in a restaurant or bar with Germans in traditional Bavarian costumes at one table, and next to them are Senegalese fans beating on African drums, and it's all love! Throughout this book, I will refer to the beautiful game as "*football.*" I am not talking about the National Football League (NFL) football, the most popular sport in the USA. I prefer to call that sport "hand-egg" or "hand-oval."

The mass appeal of the World Cup is unlike anything else. Over 1 billion people watch the World Cup. The World Cup unites people across cultural, religious, and political divides. Attending World Cups made me realize that generally, people don't have a problem with each other; governments do.

My First World Cup: Recounting Personal Experiences and Emotions from My First World Cup

Before I can talk about my first World Cup experience, I must share some key moments of my planning—or lack of planning. When I learned that the 2010 World Cup was to be hosted in South Africa, it was music to my ears. I have always wanted to visit Africa, and I was looking to combine my love for football with my strong desire to visit.

The Vegas Connection: A Last-Minute Miracle

I was in Las Vegas in May 2010. I had secured a ticket for a semi-final match in Durban, South Africa, and my flight from Las Vegas to Atlanta to Johannesburg, South Africa, was two weeks away. I hadn't taken into account a "minor" part of my trip… accommodation. I knew I was going, and figuring out where I would lay my head at night would work itself out. Being so close to my travel date with no confirmed lodging was not a good idea, especially considering the high demand during the World Cup.

I was visiting a fraternity brother (Omega Psi Phi Fraternity, Inc.) at his house when I mentioned that I didn't have a place to stay in Johannesburg (Joburg). It turns out his wife was from Kenya, and his wife's college roommate was living in Joburg. They said they would contact her to see if she would be willing to host me and let me stay at her place during my trip. A few days passed, and my frat brother contacted me, telling me that Faith, his wife's former roommate in Joburg, was on board with hosting me as her guest during the World Cup. I needed this good news! I got Faith's contact information, and we sorted out the details. I was ready to go to my first World Cup!

I was on a work trip at Tyndall Air Force Base, Florida, and I had to cut the trip short to get back to Las Vegas and catch my flight to South Africa on June 25th. Before I left Florida for Vegas to catch my flight, everything at work came to a standstill because the USA vs. Algeria game was on. I remember being with a large group of Airmen in the squadron bar, anxiously watching the game and rooting for Team USA. Then, one of the sweetest World Cup memories happened. Landon Donovan scored the last-second game-winning goal. The place erupted and went wild in celebration. The USA moved on to the Round of 16.

This dramatic late goal put me on such a high, and I couldn't believe I would be in South Africa enjoying the World Cup in less than forty-eight hours! Although my match tickets were for a much later game in the tournament, I knew the vibes and atmosphere at bars and restaurants would be great. Besides, I would be in Africa, the motherland, for the first time. At that time, I still knew nothing about FIFA Fan Fest and Fan Zones.

Wings of Determination

My flight to Atlanta from Las Vegas was uneventful. While on a long layover in Atlanta, I got a text from Faith, my host, "Hi Paul. Would you like tickets for the USA vs. Ghana game?" I couldn't believe what I was reading. Would I like tickets?! Can fish swim!??! I responded, "YES!" Our flight was scheduled to land in Joburg at 5 PM, and the game started at 8:30 PM. Faith said she would iron out the details and let me know when I arrived in Joburg.

Next, it was time to board my flight. This flight, DL 200, is Delta Airlines' longest route by time at 16 hours. I was not balling out in first class, but I did select a window seat in the front row of my section, so I had unrestricted legroom and didn't have to climb over anyone to get up and go to the bathroom. This was my first time flying on a Boeing 777, which was the largest twin-engine commercial airplane at the time.

Suddenly, it got dark while we were boarding, and baggage handlers loaded the luggage onto the aircraft. Mean-looking dark gray clouds moved above the airport, and rain started pouring. There was rain, lightning, wind, and thunder. Things were not looking good, and there was no movement on the ramp. The airport was at a standstill. Next, we heard the infamous announcement that no passenger wants to hear after the boarding doors have been closed. The pilot's voice came over the PA system and told us that severe weather had shut down the airfield, and we had to wait for the storm to pass.

I was getting nervous. We were to land in Joburg at 5 PM, and the game started at 8:30 PM. According to Google Maps, the drive from the Airport in Joburg to Rustenburg, the game's location, was about two hours. I also had to factor in the time to clear customs and retrieve my luggage. I was getting sad with each minute that ticked by during the delay. Was I going to miss my shot at going to a World Cup game as soon as I arrived in South Africa? I was ready to squeeze a single tear from my right eye like Denzel Washington's character in *Glory*.

After about 30 minutes, the pilot came on the PA again and told us he was coordinating with the FAA and Delta Operations Center to get our flight clearance out of Atlanta. Thirty minutes later, the pilot announced that we got clearance. As the massive General Electric 777 engines started,

I looked out the window; it was still raining, and no other aircraft were taxiing, landing, or taking off. Interesting.

A massive storm wall off the East Coast stretched from New York down to the tip of Florida. The pilot explained that he got special permission to take off. Instead of flying east toward South Africa, we would fly south toward the southern tip of Florida before turning east for South Africa. Fortunately, we were on a 777. The plane had plenty of gas to execute this "minor" weather detour.

This single Delta Airlines 777 taxied to the active runway and blasted off from ATL airport while the airfield was at a complete standstill. I kept looking at the time. The World Clock on my phone showed me the time in SA, and I kept doing the math in my head for when we would land and when the game would start.

The long flight allowed World Cup travelers and fans on the plane to become acquainted. Everyone excitedly discussed the USA vs. Algeria game and the dramatic late winning goal. The atmosphere on the plane was festive. I was stretching my legs and taking a stroll on the flight when I met Miguel. Miguel was Venezuelan, loved football, and was just as excited as I was about going to the World Cup. I told him about the game tickets I'd be getting for the USA vs. Ghana game. Miguel said he had nothing going on when he arrived in South Africa and asked if he could tag along for the trip to Rustenburg for the game. I said sure! But I had no idea how I was getting there and would find out and figure it out when we landed.

Since I was seated in the front of my plane section, the flight attendant's jump seat was directly in front of me. I go through a few rum and Coke cocktails on the long flight. I got to know my section's flight attendant well as she passed me the cocktails. I told her about the USA vs. Ghana game starting soon after we landed and how I had gotten tickets. "Do you want to know why we were the only aircraft that took off out of Atlanta?" I said 'sure, please share.' She responded, "The pilots have tickets for the game too!"

Strangers, Luggage, Luck, and the Game: From the Airport to the Stadium

Landing after being airborne for over sixteen hours (more like seventeen hours after the detour around Florida) was such a sweet feeling. I was officially in Africa for the first time! I was excited. Oh yeah, I was about to be handed tickets for my first-ever World Cup match, starting a few hours after I walked off the plane!

The Airport was decked out and decorated with many World Cup displays, photos, booths, etc.; this warm welcome to South Africa and the World Cup in the airport added to the excitement. I texted Faith while I got off the plane. I went through customs, retrieved my baggage, got some cash from an ATM, and freshened up a bit in a bathroom. She texted me back with what parking lot to find her, and that's where I headed.

Miguel was with me when I met Faith for the first time, and I introduced him to her. She introduced us to Andile, our driver to Rustenburg. We loaded our luggage into her car, which she was going to take home with her. Then she gave me a crisp, shiny match ticket. A huge smile took over my face. It was my first time seeing and holding a physical ticket for a World Cup game. I gave her a huge hug!

With limited time available, since Rustenburg was nearly two hours away, we said our goodbyes, climbed into the cars and hit the road. One hour after I landed in a new continent and country, I tossed all my luggage into the car of a stranger I just met, got into a car with a driver I had just met, with a dude I met on the flight. You couldn't make this stuff up. What could have gone wrong?

My excitement was immeasurable when we arrived in Rustenburg. When we got the first glimpse of the massive stadium and the lighting, I was even more excited. Then we hit traffic—lots of it. The game had already started. During the drive, we put a plan together. Miguel and the driver would find a nearby bar or restaurant to watch the game, and I would find them afterward. We were close enough to the stadium where I could hear the vuvuzela horns blowing, but the traffic was at a standstill.

Vuvuzelas, long plastic horns used by football fans in South Africa, had received negative attention from the media during the World Cup. But to me, the sound of thousands of vuvuzelas was incredible. Impatiently, I hopped out of the car and walked to the stadium. I found my gate, etc., and entered the stadium.

One of my favorite parts of going to a football game is arriving at my section and walking through the tunnel to get to my row and seat. This is where you get your first full view of the field and the size of the massive sold-out stadium. It was amazing to see the perfectly manicured field, crisp white lines, the bright lights, thousands of fans, and hear the crowd's roar mixed with the vuvuzela horns. I made it! I wanted to pinch myself. I no longer had to dream about what it was like to attend a World

Cup game. My seat was excellent, too! I was in the corner right by the corner kick flag, about five rows from the field. The game was in the 37th minute. I finally achieved my goal and dream, which started in Kingston, Jamaica, in 1986. I was at a World Cup match.

The Planning Stages: Essential Steps and Considerations for Planning a World Cup Trip

Attending the World Cup will cost money; make no mistake about that. However, with proper planning, you do not have to go broke attending the World Cup. I will outline ways to minimize your expenses when attending the World Cup. But first, we must do some financial housekeeping.

If I had consumer debt, I would have no business attending the World Cup. I would pay off my debt first. I couldn't fully enjoy the World Cup, knowing I had just racked up another $5,000 to $10,000 in debt. Do not put yourself in a bad financial position to attend the World Cup. Four years is plenty of time to get your money right and enjoy the world's ultimate sporting spectacle with financial peace of mind.

The first significant question to ask yourself is, "How much do I want to spend?" The beauty of the World Cup being every four years is that it gives you four years to create your budget and save money. I firmly believe in building lasting, rich memories over buying things. Making meaningful experiences helps to make you happy. Buying things does not.

Open an online high-yield savings account (HYSA). I use Capital One's HYSA for all my savings goals. Many banks, especially online banks with low or little overhead expenses, offer HYSAs with reasonable interest rates. Alternatives include Ally Bank and SoFi. Name your HYSA "World Cup." Connect your World Cup account to your primary checking account, where you receive your monthly income. Set up an automatic transfer each month to your World Cup account. Set it and forget it.

The earlier you start funding your World Cup account, the less money you will have to save each month. If your savings rate is high enough each month, just the interest alone for three years can cover a game ticket. Personal finance is personal; save whatever you comfortably can each month. If you are committed to attending the World Cup like a pro, you will be serious about saving as much money as possible. You may have to cut unnecessary expenses and redirect those savings toward your World Cup account.

Don't be like me leading up to South Africa 2010. You should have your accommodation lined up much earlier than 2 weeks before your flight. The significant expenses, as with most international trips, will be airfare (to the country and within the country), lodging, and game tickets, depending on how many or the scope of the games you attend. If you attend the Opening game and the Final, you will pay more for those two tickets than tickets for five games in the opening round.

The second significant question is, "How long do I want to be at the World Cup?" The best answer is, "I want to attend the entire World Cup!" That's a whole month. Unless you stay with someone for free, lodging costs add up the longer you are at the World Cup. I've been to four World Cups but have never stayed for an entire one. Now that I am retired, I plan to attend a World Cup from start to finish.

I've done two to two-and-a-half weeks for my World Cup trips. For South Africa 2010, I was there in the second half of the tournament. For Brazil 2014, I was there for the first half (Being in Sao Palo for the opener in Brazil was a memorable experience. The host nation always plays in the opening game). For Russia 2018, I was there for the second half of the tournament. For Qatar 2022, I was there at the first half, but not at the exact start of the tournament.

Fourteen to seventeen days aligned best with my finances, and I had a job to return to. I was planning for Qatar 2022 while I was still in the Air Force (I retired in 2021), and since I was not planning the trip with a retirement mindset, I defaulted to my usual two-and-a-half-ish-week trip. However long your stay, being at the World Cup for the front end of the tournament vs. the back end makes a huge difference.

Here are some pros of being there at the start of the tournament:

- Everyone is there! Fans from all nations are present and the energy is high. If you like meeting people and fans from all over the world, this is the time to be there. Taking pictures with fans from around the world is an incredible experience. I took a picture with a fan once, and he told me he was working on getting a picture with a fan from every nation in the World Cup. That was a cool idea that I will try at my next World Cup. You should, too!

- If your team is not a football powerhouse, your best bet is to attend the group stage games to guarantee you see your team play. If your team progresses in the tournament, you may have to call your boss and extend your trip.

- Games, games, and more games! There are games all day, every day, during the front end of the tournament. You can spend your entire day at the FIFA Fan Fest watching games. I will explain what a Fan Fest is later.

- Since many matches occur in the Group Stage, getting tickets involves less hassle. More games mean more tickets and more chances to get tickets for games.

- Ticket prices are much lower in the World Cup's group stage because there are so many games in this stage.

Here are some of the pros of attending the World Cup during the second half of the tournament:

- Fewer games. On days that have one or no games, you get time for some touristy stuff. The World Cup can be so polarizing that you may forget you are in an amazing country with tons of cool things to do and see. Take advantage of the lighter match schedule and do some sightseeing.

- When a powerhouse team loses and gets eliminated from the tournament, their disappointed fans tend to unload tons of tickets for matches they anticipated for bargain prices. When a favored team exits the tournament, this is a good time to closely monitor the FIFA ticket resale portal and immediately snag a resale ticket when it becomes available. If you meet the right fan, they may even give away unwanted tickets for future games as they plan to depart the country with their favorite team.

- You get to see the best teams play against each other. If you want the best bang for your buck, the second half of the tournament features the strongest teams. You get to watch some of the best teams going head-to-head. You may also get to watch surprise dark horse teams, like Morocco in Qatar 2022.

- More lodging options. When major teams are eliminated, the team leaves, and so do many of their disappointed fans. This mass exodus of fans and teams frees up lodging at hotels, Airbnb, etc. You need to act quickly to take advantage of this brief availability of lodging options since more fans will still be flying in for the winning teams' next game. I saw this happen in

Qatar. As Morocco advanced further in the tournament, more Morocco fans arrived.

- If the host nation progresses further into the tournament, you get to experience an entire nation catch a case of World Cup fever. From my experience, the overall World Cup vibe is extra-incredible when the host nation wins games and advances through the tournament. Even if they are not football fans, it seems as if the locals living in the host country get more excited and interested with every win.

I watched Russia eliminate Spain at the Red Square FIFA Fanfest during the Russia 2018 World Cup. The entire nation erupted into celebration. It was as if every Russian was in the streets of Moscow singing and celebrating their big win. It was a fantastic experience I will never forget!

I had a similar experience in South Africa in 2010. Africa supported Ghana, which meant the host nation supported Ghana. It was a beautiful thing to behold and experience. It was so intoxicating that it would have been hard not to support Ghana if you were a neutral fan.

You can also attend in the middle of the tournament to catch the end of the Group Stage, Round of 16, and quarter-finals. A popular football online forum conducted a poll before the Qatar 2022 World Cup. The poll asked, "At what stage(s) of the tournament will you be in Qatar?" 181 people responded. 87% were there for the Group Stage. 40% were there for the Round of 16. 22.6% were there for the quarter-finals and semi-finals. 24% were there for the final. These poll results make sense. If you want to be guaranteed to see your team play, arrive at the start of the tournament. You get to watch the Group Stage matches and enjoy the festivities with fans of all participating nations.

This chapter explored the overall international appeal of the World Cup, which explains why a global audience of 1.5 billion people watched the 2022 World Cup final match. I shared some of my experiences and lessons from my 2010 World Cup trip to South Africa. Lastly, we discussed why understanding the fan experience of the World Cup's beginning, middle, and end can help you plan your trip and manage expectations. Now that those major planning considerations are understood, let's acquire match tickets.

Mastering the FIFA World Cup Ticket Game

Getting your hands on tickets for a World Cup match can be as thrilling as the match itself. This is because acquiring a ticket is no easy task. This chapter will explore the various ways to secure your spot in the stands, from official FIFA channels to purchasing from third parties. We will also discuss the different ticket categories and their prices. Understanding these nuances will make you a more informed fan when shopping for tickets.

Securing Tickets: Strategies for Obtaining Tickets, Including Official Channels and Resale Markets

Getting tickets for World Cup matches is crucial for attending the World Cup. Getting a match ticket directly from FIFA is no easy task. There is an incredibly high demand for match tickets. Millions of fans are trying to buy tickets for limited seats. FIFA releases tickets for sale in phases. Even if you apply, you are not guaranteed to get tickets.

According to some World Cup discussion boards, the success rate of getting a ticket is about 6% - 10%, depending on the demand for the matches you apply for. FIFA's website can become overwhelmed when tickets go on sale, leading to crashes, errors, and long wait times. Be patient. Keep applying.

Apply for multiple matches and ticket categories to increase your chances.

The first step to getting World Cup tickets is to visit FIFA's website, create an account, and go to their ticketing portal. Sign up for notifications for ticket sales and updates. You will receive a notification when tickets are on sale. World Cup tickets go on sale in phases, with the first phase usually starting in October, the year before the tournament begins.

In previous World Cups, Phase One was a random lottery before the qualified teams (except for the host nation team(s)) were confirmed. Phase Two is first come, first served after the group draw is determined. Phase Three is another random lottery, and Phase Four is first come, first served - if necessary. Purchasing tickets through FIFA is the official and recommended way to buy tickets; you should use this option because you are guaranteed entry into the stadium with tickets purchased through FIFA.

You can bid for stadium-specific tickets. This ticket bidding option is excellent if you want to stay in one location during your trip without flying around to watch different games in different stadiums. With this ticket option, you get tickets to whatever games take place in the stadium you choose.

You can also bid for team-specific tickets. These tickets allow you to watch your team wherever and whenever they play during the tournament. If your team makes it out of the first round, this is the perfect way to follow them around the host country.

You can buy match-specific tickets. This ticket sales type is the most interesting because when you purchase the ticket, you have no idea who will be playing in the game, and you won't know until the tournament gets to the match number. For South Africa 2010, I was fortunate enough to get tickets to match #62. This was the semi-final match between Germany and Spain in Durban's Moses Mabhida Stadium (Spain won 1 - 0). The cool part about this ticket-buying option is that if watching the opening or the final match is your priority, you make your travel arrangements super early. The opening match and final dates are set when the World Cup tournament dates are released. If you plan your trip earlier, you can save a lot of money.

FIFA partners with corporate affiliates in the travel and hospitality industry. According to The World Cup Guide (2024), you can skip the line of the ticket sales phases by working with a company such as MATCH if you are willing to fork out premium dollars to get a guaranteed ticket. More information about hospitality packages is coming up in this chapter. Companies such as Next Generation International and Roadtrips also have World Cup travel packages. You will pay top dollar for these packages, but they include official World Cup tickets from FIFA.

If you or you know someone who works for an official World Cup corporate sponsor, you can access official World Cup tickets. Faith, my host when I went to South Africa in 2010, worked for a bank that was a corporate sponsor of the World Cup. She brought tickets home from work and gave me tickets every few days during the World Cup. Through this connection, I got a ticket for the final match. I gladly paid for that ticket.

The World Cup Guide (2024) also includes Team Federations as an official way to purchase World Cup tickets. FIFA gives each soccer federation tickets, and it is up to those federations to manage and distribute their ticket allotments. Contact your nation's football federation for details about their World Cup ticket allocation.

To protect World Cup attendees, FIFA advises against buying tickets via third-party sellers. The unauthorized reselling of tickets is a violation of FIFA's general terms. Fake tickets and scams are also a valid concern. Fortunately, I have never dealt with scammers when purchasing tickets from third parties during the World Cup. If you are more comfortable buying third-party tickets through FIFA, its ticketing portal allows tickets to be resold with peace of mind. I used this portal for Qatar 2022.

If a ticket for a big game is available, it will be purchased within seconds of being listed on the resale portal. You must stare at your phone and keep refreshing the site, hoping for a resale ticket to become available, and immediately purchase it. There are reputable resale platforms, but FIFA does not condone this practice. Beware of scams (the ticket price may be too good to be true) or ridiculous price markups.

Various online forums, Facebook groups, Reddit, and reputable ticket resale sites exist. One of my best sources for getting tickets and keeping up with everything before, during, and after the World Cup is Bigsoccer.com, where fans at the World Cup buy and sell tickets. This forum has been helpful because the rules mandate that tickets be sold at face value, keeping away sharks with ridiculously marked-up ticket prices.

While in Qatar, I responded to a random post in a World Cup Facebook group. Someone on the thread asked if I was in

Qatar and said that she wanted to come to Qatar from the United Arab Emirates to see a game, but she did not know how to get tickets. I told her I was in touch with someone with an extra ticket for a few games (I found this ticket seller on Bigsoccer.com). I got her in touch with the seller, and she flew in. She attended her first World Cup game with the guy who sold her the ticket on her first day at the tournament. Later, we all linked up at a restaurant, ate, got to know each other, and watched a game together. A few days later, I went to see a game with the same guy because I also purchased a ticket from him. I'm still friends with both.

Hopefully, I'm doing a decent job explaining that getting match tickets at the World Cup is possible once you are in the host nation with an open mind and a flexible schedule. It was easier for me since I was solo and had a flexible schedule. Many ticket sellers had a pair of tickets and were trying to sell one. Oftentimes, I had to pass on tickets because the seller wanted to sell both tickets as a pair.

A game ticket is required to get an official FIFA Fan ID/Visa for the Russia and Qatar tournaments. Russia 2018, for example, required you to have a match ticket before you could apply for a FIFA Fan ID. The FIFA Fan ID was also my entry Visa into Russia. It also meant free travel on designated trains between host cities on match days and free public transportation in host cities on match days.

I met a gentleman from the USA in St. Petersburg, Russia. He was from Minnesota and not a football fan. He told me he got a game ticket to get a Fan ID to visit Russia without applying for a standard tourist visa. Most World Cup host nations also allow the Fan ID/Visa to remain active for a few months after the World Cup. Qatar's Hayya card/visa allowed visitors to stay in the country until January 23rd, 2023. It was possible to stay and get your tourism on after the World Cup.

Russia 2018 was the first World Cup with the Fan ID/Visa. For Brazil 2014, if you had a match ticket, you had a "World Cup" visa. I already had an active visa for Brazil in 2014, so getting there without a match ticket was not an issue for me. For South Africa in 2010, there was no visa requirement for me since I have a US passport.

Qatar 2022 took things to another level using technology. Qatar had a World Cup app to get your Hayya Card, the mandatory Fan ID. Requirements were a match ticket, confirmed accommodation in Qatar, and a valid passport. Once I got my Hayya card (electronic in my app), it became my Visa, allowing me to enter Qatar. It also allowed me to

Paul Prosper

travel for free on public transportation during the tournament, and it was required for stadium and Fan Festival entry.

Initially, you could not get into Qatar without a match ticket and a Hayya card. The previous three host nations, before Qatar, allowed you to fly in with a standard visa and then get a match ticket once you were in the country. Qatar's Ministry of Interior removed the game ticket requirement to obtain a Hayya card/visa a few days before the tournament started, but lodging verification was still required (Fragomen, 2022). World Cup 2026 may have something similar to allow fans to enter the USA, Mexico, and Canada via their Fan ID/Visa.

Lastly, scalpers sell tickets outside the stadium before kick-off. It's good practice to have the scalper walk with you to the turnstiles where the ticket is scanned. That's the only way you can guarantee the ticket is valid. This practice is becoming obsolete because it is used with paper tickets.

All Qatar tickets were digital and available via the Hayya app, and it was easy to get tickets from people via the Hayya app. I did not have to physically meet the people to purchase tickets like I had to do at previous World Cups. I also did not have to worry if the electronic tickets were fake. If a ticket was in the app, it was official, and you were good to go.

42

Though I do not recommend this, here's how I secured a ticket or four in Qatar. I would find a post in an online forum, contact the person selling a ticket for a match I wanted to see, exchange numbers, and text them via WhatsApp. We would agree on the ticket price (hopefully no more than face value). I would pay via PayPal and share my email address connected to the Hayya app. The app would notify me that the seller was sending tickets, and I could accept or reject them. When I hit accept, the ticket was instantly downloaded in the Hayya app on my phone. During previous World Cups, you had to be in the same city as the seller so you could meet face-to-face to finalize the deal and get the physical ticket.

This ticket-purchasing method allowed me to apply for my Qatar visa. I had no luck getting a ticket through the FIFA website. A friend in Atlanta was fortunate enough to secure a few tickets, so I bought one from him. Even though he was in Atlanta and I was in Jamaica, the ticket appeared in the app on my phone within minutes. Qatar 2022 changed the game, making it much easier to buy tickets from anyone, anywhere with a ticket for sale.

I know what you are thinking. This method of buying a ticket is crazy! How do you know that the seller is legit and not a scammer? After being in World Cup forums for over 16 years, I've gotten to know people and can also check their profiles, see how long they have been on the forum, how active they are, etc.

If anyone is scamming people in the forum, they will be reported and removed. It has never happened to me. So far, these forums have had legit fans simply trying to offload and purchase tickets. I like using PayPal because it has a pretty good dispute process if you do not get the tickets you paid for. The safest, best, and official way to purchase World Cup tickets is through FIFA.

Ticket Categories and Pricing

World Cup tickets are divided into three categories:

- *Category one* tickets are the most expensive and closest to the middle of the field, giving you that TV view of the pitch. According to the World Cup Guide (2024), you will be seated between the 18-yard box lines.

- *Category two* tickets are less expensive and generally run from the 18-yard box to the end line in the corners of the stadium.

- *Category three* tickets are the most inexpensive and will be behind the goals.

- *Category four* tickets, if available, are reserved for residents of the host nation.

I don't care where I sit as long as I am in the stadium watching the game. There's no bad seat in the stadium. For World Cup tickets, you cannot select your seats. You can only choose the categories. If you get the ticket in the category of your choice, you will have a general idea of where you will be sitting. Keep in mind that a category one ticket can put you at the top level of the stadium.

As I mentioned before, FIFA does offer hospitality packages or a premium World Cup experience that includes more than just a game ticket. Hospitality packages target businesses that want to reward employees or clients, people with high net worth, and passionate fans who want the ultimate match-day experience. Hospitality packages vary but will usually include:

- Premium seating or even watching the game in a box suite with food and beverages included.

- Private lounges where you can relax in luxury with dedicated service.

- Meet-and-greet events where you can meet football legends and current players.

- VIP access: Get in and out of the stadium quickly with little to no waiting in queues.

- Entertainment options to enhance your match day experience pre- and post-match.

For the first time, during Qatar 2022, FIFA allocated tickets for disabled fans and those with limited mobility across five categories: wheelchair users, easy access amenity, easy access standard, easy access extra-width, and sensory rooms. All these tickets (except for easy access extra-width) come with a complimentary ticket for a companion. Hopefully, FIFA will continue to offer this ticket type, enabling disabled fans to attend and enjoy World Cup games in person.

Now that you know how to get tickets and the different categories of tickets, how much do World Cup tickets cost? Ticket prices vary. If you execute the high-yield savings account monthly saving strategy I mentioned earlier, you should have funds to purchase multiple game tickets. Look at the table below with Russia 2018 ticket prices in US dollars. While I expect future World Cup ticket prices to be higher due to inflation, the table below gives a general idea of how the ticket pricing structure works.

Match(es)	Category 1	Category 2	Category 3
Opening Match	$550	$390	$220
Group Stage	$210	$165	$115
Round of 16	$245	$185	$115
Quarter-Finals	$365	$255	$175
Semi-Finals	$750	$480	$285
3rd Place Match	$365	$255	$175
Final	$1,100	$710	$455

With multiple ways to secure tickets for the World Cup, it's advisable to get them as early as you can so you can complete your Fan ID/Visa process upfront. Good luck bidding for tickets on the FIFA website. If you fail to secure a ticket through official channels, you can still get tickets through third parties. In most cases, you must obtain your first ticket through official channels or from someone who did, to allow you to apply for your visa/FIFA fan ID.

Planes, Trains, and Automobiles: Transportation Tips for World Cup Fans

How will you get to the World Cup? Hopefully, it will come to your country, so you won't have to handle the numerous transportation and logistics challenges of attending in a foreign nation. Transportation is typically the second largest expense after lodging when traveling internationally for the World Cup. This chapter will examine transportation options to reach the World Cup, during your time there, and travel considerations that can enhance your journey and overall experience at the event.

Transportation Options: Exploring Various Transportation Options – Flights, Trains, and Buses

Here's how I get to the host nation from my home country. I have been flying Delta Airlines for over 20 years and use their American Express Platinum credit card. Since the World Cup is every four years, I use that time to accrue enough SkyMiles to cover my round-trip flight to the World Cup. While I was at World Cup 2014, I was using my SkyMiles credit card and accruing SkyMiles for my flight to World Cup 2018. I am not a fan of debt. You shouldn't be, either. Please do not go into debt using this method. If you use your credit card for miles, please pay off your credit card monthly so you do not carry or build up a balance.

One of the tenets of building wealth is to avoid debt. If you do not have the discipline to pay off your credit card balance each month, do not use this method. I have witnessed people go into significant debt trying to accrue SkyMiles and credit card reward points. Do not fall into this trap. Check out *thepointsguy.com* for information and tips on maximizing credit card and loyalty reward points.

If you are not loyal to any airline and want to get there as cheaply as possible, check out going.com. Other websites offer competitive low fares for international flights, such as Cheap Tickets, CheapOair, Cheapflights, Google Flights, etc. Many websites will notify you when a deal is available on a flight to your desired World Cup destination.

There is another way to fly to the World Cup at a low or no cost: by using non-revenue friends and family airline travel options. Think carefully. Who do you know that works for a major airline? If you're fortunate enough to have such a connection in the airline industry, you might be in luck!

First, you need to understand the nature of flying standby. It isn't for everyone. Flexibility is key because seats on the plane may not be available, or you could be bumped off the flight at the last minute. This happens because priority levels determine who can board the flight before or after you as a non-revenue passenger. For instance, airline employees and their immediate family members traveling to the World Cup will have a higher priority than you if you're using a friends and family buddy pass.

Competition for non-revenue seats on flights to the World Cup will be intense! Stay flexible. Stay patient. Be ready to buy a full-price ticket if necessary. Be prepared to book a hotel for an extra night and try again the next day. Consider flying in before the World Cup and leaving well after it when flight demand decreases. You may still need to cover taxes and fees for your seat. Don't forget to bring back a World Cup gift for the airline employee who helped you secure the non-revenue seat.

I waited until I finalized my accommodation booking and received my Visa to enter Qatar before contacting Delta Airlines for my award-travel round-trip flight. Unfortunately, I was too late, and there were no award-travel seats to Doha and back to Jamaica. For this World Cup, my SkyMiles only covered me from Montego Bay to New York City and then from New York City to Paris.

On the return trip, SkyMiles only covered me from Paris to New York City and from New York City to Montego Bay. I had to pay for the Paris to Qatar portion of the trip. That was my first time in four World Cups paying airfare to get to the World Cup. I'll never make that mistake again; those flights were expensive!

Inquire with your preferred airline on the earliest you can book a flight for your travel dates. In my case, I asked Delta Airlines about the earliest I could redeem miles for a flight to the World Cup host nation. Booking your flight as early as possible is crucial, especially if you redeem loyalty points or miles. Airlines only allow so many award travelers on these routes.

Depending on the games you want to attend and the size of the host nation, your flight travel may not end when you arrive in-country. For example, during the 2014 World Cup in Brazil, I caught 14 flights. I learned just how massive Brazil is during this trip. During South Africa 2010, I flew to Cape Town twice from Joburg and once to Durban for a match. That's six flights plus the epic road trip to Rustenburg when I landed in South Africa.

I've been to two World Cups in huge countries (Russia and Brazil), one medium-sized country (South Africa), and one tiny country (Qatar). Qatar was convenient due to its size. I stayed in one location, and every stadium was within a 30-minute Uber drive. There was no need to fly anywhere during Qatar 2022. However, I did fly to Dubai for a quick 3-day trip during Qatar 2022. The World Cup watch parties in Dubai were epic!

Qatar exceeded expectations to guarantee that World Cup fans had a positive experience. Qatar 2022 was the first World Cup I attended; if you had tickets, you could attend multiple matches in a single day and catch all the games without missing a single minute. After the games, buses were ready to take fans, free of charge, to the stadium where the next game was held.

I prefer World Cups in small countries. Getting to the stadiums and Fan Zones is much easier. However, due to its size, lodging in Qatar was a huge problem. Airbnb properties were expensive, and the price gouging was ridiculous. However, those properties were still eventually booked because Qatar was out of accommodation. This lack of affordable accommodation was a huge problem. It was so bad that Qatar brought in three massive MSC cruise ships to accommodate fans. These three ships docked in Doha. To make things even more challenging, Qatar required proof of confirmed lodging to get your Fan ID/Hayya Card.

Country sizes impact your World Cup experience. Russia is not a tiny country; it has 11 different time zones, and World Cup stadiums are spread all over the country. For my trip, I was based in Moscow, a fantastic city. I took a train to St. Petersburg from Moscow to see the Sweden vs. Switzerland Round of 16 match (Sweden won 1- 0). I was looking forward to my overnight eight-hour train ride across Russia. I had never done an overnight train ride with beds and roommates, so this experience was unique.

My sleeper car featured four beds, and I shared this car with three other strangers. Nobody spoke to each other, which was good since I was the only non-Russian in our sleeper car. The train ride was an incredible experience, and I enjoyed the views of the Russian countryside in the morning. The temperature in St. Petersburg was much cooler than in Moscow, and there was snow on the ground in some areas during the train ride. The architecture of the buildings and canals throughout St. Petersburg reminded me of many European cities. It is beautiful, and I'm glad I took the trip.

For domestic travel during the World Cup, do your research. What are the public transportation options? Is there a subway or Metro? Buses? Trams? Uber or a ride-share service? Consider getting a travel pass if there is a Metro or Bus service. Fortunately, during Russia 2018 and Qatar 2022, fans with Fan IDs could ride the Metro for free. It was such a convenience after attending three World Cups without free transportation provided for fans. If you don't want to get a travel pass, there's no problem. Most of the World Cup cities are walkable and have convenient transportation options.

Other Travel Considerations for Your World Cup Trip

Travel Insurance: Unexpected events can occur during the World Cup. Fortunately, nothing has happened to me that has required canceling or cutting a trip short due to an emergency. Travel insurance is essential for unexpected life events before or during your trip. Medical insurance is another reasonable consideration to make before your trip. Contact your insurance provider and inquire if and how you will be covered during your trip.

Pack light! Airline luggage fees can be insane. What do they expect us to do? Fly without luggage? For Qatar 2022, I could only get to Paris using my Delta SkyMiles. My next flight to Amsterdam was with Air France, and they hit me with an overweight luggage fee of one hundred Euros. I was barely over the limit. The gate agent was very friendly, and she helped me cut off the twisty tie lock on my luggage and let me try to move stuff from my suitcase to my carry-on. Unfortunately, I could not get my suitcase under the required weight.

Though Air France, a Delta Airlines partner, did not acknowledge my platinum status with Delta regarding my luggage weight, Air France did honor my status with Delta, and I was able to spend a few hours of my layover in their First-Class Lounge at Charles de Gaulle Airport. It was a lovely lounge. My goal was to consume one hundred Euros worth of food and alcoholic beverages during my layover in their lounge, and I think I was successful. Packing light can save you money when traveling to the World Cup. I ensured Air France did not charge me for overweight luggage on my return trip.

So, what should you bring to the World Cup? The World Cup usually lasts from early June to early July. In the northern hemisphere, that's summer; in the southern hemisphere, it's winter. The weather was chilly in South Africa in 2010 because the country is far south. Be sure you understand the weather in the host nation during the World Cup and pack accordingly.

- Comfortable shoes: You will be walking a lot at the World Cup, so make sure you have comfortable shoes that will allow you to explore the city, fan zones, stadiums, etc.

- Comfortable clothing: You need a light jacket for the flight and chilly nights in the host nation. Wear layers. You may leave your room at 10 AM and stay out enjoying World Cup nightlife well after midnight. You may need to remove a layer when it warms up in the afternoon and put it back on later that night.

- Fan gear: Whether your favorite national team is in the World Cup or not, represent where you are from. I always represent Jamaica at the World Cup with scarves, jackets, etc. I also bring a USA shirt and purchase football T-shirts for all the African teams in the World Cup. Bring a flag and show it off at the World Cup; represent your nation(s).

- Power outlet adapter: These are handy in hotels and Airbnbs with international power outlets. They allow you to plug in and use your electronics.

- Portable phone charger: You can be away from your lodging for twelve hours while enjoying the World Cup. Therefore, carry a portable power bank for your phone.

- FIFA Fan ID/VISA & Passport: These are self-explanatory; without them, you probably won't even be able to check into your flight at the airport.

- FIFA Game tickets. Thank goodness Qatar raised the bar with an app for the Fan ID and game tickets. Now, you don't have to worry about packing these unless you forget to pack your phone. The app is another reason why it is essential to have a portable charger. You don't want your phone, with your tickets and Fan ID, dying on your way to the stadium.

- Camera: Unless you are a professional photographer, your phone camera is enough to capture unforgettable memories at the World Cup.

Now that you are all packed for your trip, let's discuss your flight. Getting to the World Cup can make or break your World Cup experience. My flight from Atlanta to

Johannesburg for the 2010 World Cup was about 17 hours long. That's a long time on a plane! My trip to Qatar in 2022 included five cities: Montego Bay, Atlanta, Paris, Amsterdam, and Doha. This trip was just shy of 24 hours. My total flight time from Colorado to Los Angeles to Moscow in 2018 was about 20 hours. The total flight time from Colorado to Atlanta to Sao Paolo was about 13 hours. These total flight times do not include layovers in the airport. Here are some tips to help make your long-haul flight to the World Cup more enjoyable.

- A travel pillow provides much-needed neck support and comfort.

- An eye mask and ear plugs block light and noise to help you sleep or relax.

- I've heard horror stories about blankets on planes that are never cleaned or changed between flights. Consider bringing your own to keep you warm and comfortable on the long flight.

- I have never tried compression socks for a flight, but I hear they are great for blood circulation, which can help reduce discomfort in your legs and feet.

- Wear comfortable, loose clothing. Do not wear a belt or anything that can dig into your skin while seated on your long flight.

- Noise-canceling headphones are a huge game-changer on flights. Even if I'm not listening to anything, I turn on the noise-canceling feature on my headphones for a much quieter flight.

- Carry a reusable water bottle. Just make sure it is empty when you go through security.

- Get up and move around on the flight. When I met Miguel on my flight to South Africa, I was taking a walk. You will meet and mingle with other fans going to the World Cup, especially if you wear football-related gear on the flight.

What about in-flight entertainment and productivity?

- I use long flights as a chance to do some cell phone maintenance. Is your phone running out of storage space? A long flight is a great time to delete the photos and videos that take up valuable space on your phone. Doing this on your flight frees up valuable space for the fantastic pictures and videos you will take at the World Cup.

- I also use my time on flights to maintain my phone contacts. I scroll through my contacts and delete those I no longer need or use. I also use this to create a calendar reminder to call contacts I haven't talked to in a while, or I'll draft an email and hit send when I'm back on the ground, and my phone is back on a network.

- Bring a physical book with you to read. If there is no WiFi or your gadget's batteries are dead, your physical book will come in handy. If you listen to audiobooks, download one or two to your phone or tablet to listen to them offline. You can also do this with YouTube videos and podcasts you wish to enjoy without a network connection.

- A travel journal and pen come in handy so you can jot down your thoughts. These journal entries might be helpful when writing a book about your World Cup experience one day.

- Bluetooth adapter: I will try this gadget on my next long flight. It is an adapter that you plug into the headphone jack of the inflight entertainment system. Once it is plugged in, you connect your Bluetooth headphones to it, and you can listen to in-flight movies, etc., on your headphones. Your headphones are most likely more comfortable and better quality than the headphones the airline offers.

According to an article published in the National Library of Medicine (2011), Jet lag, also known as circadian desynchrony, is a mismatch between the body's natural rhythm and your environment. This sleep disorder is due to a rapid transit across multiple time zones. Symptoms include fatigue, insomnia, difficulty concentrating, and irritability. I bring up jet lag because I don't want jet lag to hinder you and have you sleeping for two days when you arrive at the World Cup. I want you to hit the ground running like I did when I went to South Africa in 2010. I don't recall jet lag ever being an issue upon my arrival at any of the World Cups I have been to. However, we are all different, and jet lag is something to consider. Here are some ways to minimize your jet lag.

- Adjust your sleep schedule a few days before your trip. If you are going east, go to bed and wake up earlier than usual. If you are going west, go to bed and wake up later than normal. This is to get your sleep schedule as close as possible to your schedule when you arrive in the World Cup host nation.

- Stay hydrated and drink plenty of water to mitigate jet lag symptoms.

- Experts advise avoiding caffeine and alcohol. They can disrupt your sleep and make jet lag symptoms worse. I don't follow this on my long-haul flights.

- Get sunlight at your destination as soon as possible since sunlight helps reset your body's natural clock.

- Take a short nap at your destination. Keep it short and under thirty minutes. You don't want to knock out for 8 hours and wake up at 3 PM at your new destination. Upon arrival, a long snooze during the day will jack up your circadian rhythm and worsen your jet lag.

- Moderate exercise, such as walking, can help improve sleep quality. So, when you check into your lodging, if it's daytime, resist the urge to sleep and go for a walk.

The aim is to get on the sleep schedule of your new time zone.

- Give yourself time to adjust. If you know you get jet-lagged, fly in a few days before the first game you will be attending. An extra day or two in the host country can help you enjoy the game without dealing with jet lag.

Moscow to Nizhny: A Language of Friendship

I scored tickets for the France vs. Uruguay quarter-final game in Russia in 2018. I met the seller in a Moscow train station as she was leaving Moscow to attend a game. Naturally, I was very excited as it was a significant match. Since I had to figure out where the game was and how to get there, I got my ticket the day before the game. The game was at Nizhny Novgorod Stadium in the city of Nizhny Novgorod, called "Nizhny" for short.

Houston, we have a problem: There were no available seats on flights to Nizhny from Moscow. I went to the train station and discovered that all the trains had been sold out. At the time, I was unaware that my Fan ID gave me access to free trains to host cities. However, because of the last-minute nature of my situation, those free trains were probably full. I was in a pickle. I had a game ticket, and my duty was to be in my seat for the French and Uruguayan national anthems.

I had made friends with the staff at my hotel due to the time I spent at the lobby bar watching games, eating, and drinking. After the lobby bartender, you need to be on good terms with the hotel's concierge. I still have his contact information on my phone. Davit was a cool guy from the nation of Georgia. He spoke flawless English and pointed me to all the good restaurants in Moscow. I was well cared for when I arrived at the restaurants he'd made reservations for me.

When I told Davit about my transportation problem, he checked all his airline and train connections, and no seats were available to Nizhny. He told me about a friend who was a driver and that he could take me to Nizhny. I had not thought of driving. When I looked at Google Maps, I saw it was about a 6-hour drive from Moscow to Nizhny. The cost of the 12-hour round trip surpassed my match ticket's cost. However, how often do you get to go on a twelve-hour road trip in Russia with a stranger you cannot communicate with?

The following day, Ivan showed up bright and early at the hotel, ready to take me to Nizhny. Ivan looked like a lead character in a Russian mafia hit-man movie. He wore a leather jacket and jeans and was smoking a cigarette. His face was chiseled and hard. After we sized each other up, the concierge introduced us. Ivan did not know any English, and I didn't know Russian. I hopped in the car, buckled my seatbelt, and we were off! For the first hour, the ride was silent. I soaked in the sights of Moscow as we moved further and further away from the city center.

About three hours into the trip, we stopped at a gas station to use the bathroom and get gas and food. We were in a rural town somewhere between Moscow and Nizhny. While we ate a snack and drank a soda at a table in the gas station, we used Google Translate to chat a bit. The ice was starting to melt between us. We got back on the highway, heading east toward Nizhny. I had Google Maps open to track our progress and ensure that Ivan wouldn't take any detours.

We arrived safely in Nizhny, and we could see the enormous stadium and the lights glowing around it. FIFA does not let cars get anywhere near the stadiums on game day. Traffic was getting thick, and the match start time was approaching. Since it is my rule to be in my seat for the national anthems of all games I attend, I hopped out of the car and started speed walking/jogging towards the stadium. The walk was epic. The fans, the atmosphere, helicopters hovering above, I soaked it all in as I walked towards the massive stadium. France beat up an injury-depleted Uruguay 1-0 and moved on to the semi-finals.

I had met some folks from the USA the day before, and they told me about a restaurant in Nizhny that someone from the USA owned. They said it was a great place to eat and watch games in Nizhny. After I left the game, Ivan and I went to check out this restaurant. We ate, and then Ivan went back to the car to sleep while I watched games and enjoyed the World Cup vibe.

By the time Ivan and I got back on the road that night, you would have thought we were best friends. We exchanged Instagram pages; I was teaching him English and Jamaican patois, and he was teaching me Russian basics. He showed me pictures of his kids, and we were listening to our favorite songs on the radio and singing off-key and at the top of our lungs,

"ONE LOVE! ONE HEART! LET'S GET TOGETHER AND FEEL ALL RIGHT!"

When we finally arrived back at the hotel in Moscow in the wee hours of the early morning, it was a bittersweet farewell for the two of us. If I ever return to Russia, I must meet up and drink a Black Russian with Ivan!

Transportation presents a significant challenge not only to reach the World Cup but also during the event itself. Securing tickets for games is one obstacle, but having that ticket in your hand or on your phone isn't always the final hurdle you need to overcome. Oftentimes, more excitement and adventure lie in making your way to the stadium just in time to find your seat and enjoy the national anthems. In the next chapter, we will explore how to find the perfect place to stay during your World Cup trip.

From Hotels to Hostels: A World of World Cup Lodging Options

Finding the ideal place to call your temporary home is a crucial aspect of experiencing the World Cup like a pro. You want a location that is safe, reasonably priced, and provides easy access to public transportation and World Cup excitement. Each lodging option has its pros and cons. This chapter will explore the advantages and disadvantages of different lodging choices.

Finding the Perfect Stay: Accommodation Recommendations – Hotels, Hostels, and Local Rentals

When I started looking for places to stay for Qatar 2022 on Airbnb, I had to double-check and ensure Airbnb wasn't quoting prices in Jamaican Dollars. That's how high the prices were. They were quoted in US dollars, and I could not believe it. Book your lodging as early as possible. I'm a Hilton guy, and Hilton's website allows you to book a hotel room as early as 365 days before you arrive.

Hilton has a co-branded credit card where you can accrue points for Hilton Brand hotel stays whenever you spend using the credit card. Do not go into debt pursuing hotel points. If you stay at enough hotels during the 4 years leading up to the World Cup, you may be able to cover your entire stay or even a night's stay with your points. Redeeming points can lead to significant savings on your trip.

If you use Airbnb, you can find a host who has not yet increased their rates for the World Cup dates. If you see such an opportunity, jump on it. Hopefully, the host will not cancel your reservation to increase prices for another potential guest. This cancelation would hurt the host because Airbnb frowns on hosts canceling confirmed reservations without proper justification.

I'm a host on Airbnb, and my listing calendar allows me to set my property's booking calendar prices for up to two years. Does this mean potential guests can book two years out? I checked a random property in Miami, and Airbnb provided two years on the calendar that I could book the property. I can now book my World Cup 2026 stay in Mexico! Book your lodging as soon as possible. I can't stress this point enough. You want your accommodation close to a stadium, Fan Zone, or public transportation.

Hotels are usually and historically the first choice for most travelers when planning a trip. Here are some advantages of staying in a hotel during the World Cup:

- It's convenient, especially if you are already familiar with the brand. You know what to expect, and hotels offer many amenities that cater to your travel needs.

- Location! Hotels are usually in the middle of the action, and you are within walking distance of shops, restaurants, etc.

- Security: I am not very worried about security when I stay in a hotel. After a specific time at night, most hotels only allow entry to those with an active room key. Some hotels have security guards on the property for added security.

- Services: The hotel concierge in Russia saved the day by finding me a driver to take me to the game in Nizhny. If you have a long time before your flight after you check out, it's not a problem. Most hotels will store your luggage, and you can go to a Fan Fest or bar to enjoy the day's games without worrying about your luggage.

- If you are part of a loyalty program with a hotel brand, you can use your points to cover one night of your stay or even your entire trip, depending on how many hotel points you can amass over the four years leading up to the next World Cup.

Cons of staying in a hotel during the World Cup:

- Cost: Hotels can be expensive. Hotels drastically raise their rates during the World Cup. Even worse, some hotels will have minimum night stay packages, forcing you to pay for more nights than you may need or can afford to stay.

- Crowded: A large, popular hotel may be crowded. The lobby may look like a zoo full of people all day and night during the World Cup. Some hotel guests may not be a fan of that when simply trying to get to the elevator to get to their room. Also, these crowds may mean long lines to take a taxi, get breakfast, eat a meal at a hotel restaurant, or get another rum and coke at the hotel bar.

- If you stay in your hotel room, you can mess around and completely isolate yourself. Getting too comfy in your hotel room can cause you to miss out on exploring the city and interacting with fans and locals.

If you want an immersive cultural experience, staying in a hotel may not be the best option.

- You have to eat out every day, and eating out a few times a day can quickly rack up the cost of your trip.

- Stay away from the mini-bar in your hotel room. That can of Pepsi and a bag of chips will cost you an arm and a leg.

Airbnb (when I say Airbnb, I mean any short-term stay furnished rental property). Pros of staying in an Airbnb during the World Cup:

- More space and privacy. When you stay in an Airbnb, the pool doesn't close, your kitchen is open 24/7, and you can play your music/TV a bit louder than in a hotel. Privacy is essential if you have guests at your Airbnb. Depending on the country, many hotels require your guests to complete paperwork, provide ID, etc.

- It feels like home! You can't beat staying in a home. It feels better than being confined to a 300-square-foot hotel room. You have a living room, kitchen, and laundry room to call home during your trip.

- Cost-effective. Usually, staying in an Airbnb is less expensive than staying in a hotel. There are no phantom fees at checkout when you stay in an Airbnb. There are no pre-authorizations on your credit card that you have to wait to be refunded to your card 48 hours after checking out of an Airbnb.

- You can cook your meals, saving you a lot of money. You won't have to eat out for multiple meals every day during your trip.

- If you don't want to cook but still want to enjoy home-cooked meals, you can hire a chef to cook at your Airbnb.

- You can negotiate rates directly with the property host. Many hosts offer discounts for extended stays.

Cons of staying in an Airbnb during the World Cup

- Amenities at Airbnb may not be as pleasant as those at a hotel. For example, there will probably not be daily room service or breakfast (unless you hire a chef).

- An Airbnb increases the uncertainty factor. Issues can pop up with the property or the host. I have never done a shared Airbnb. I always rent an entire home or apartment. That's just my personal preference. Sharing a space with an owner can bring down the cost, but shared spaces increase the uncertainty factor.

- Some Airbnb hosts can get a bit carried away with what they want you to do before you check out. Be sure to read the house rules before you book. You may have to vacuum the floors, take out the trash, and wash the dishes before you check out.

- Unlike a hotel, when staying in an Airbnb, unless you are in a gated facility or a property with onsite security, you are a part of the local community without security. This is not bad, but it is something to consider depending on your security preferences when traveling. The security you get at a hotel does not exist. Do your research on where you are staying when booking an Airbnb. I like to pull up the Airbnb Map on one screen and Google Maps on another screen. This way, I can see the general location of the Airbnb and the lay of the land in the city. For example, I can see where airports, stadiums, Fan Zones, and public transportation are located before I book.

Stay with someone you know. If you are fortunate enough to crash at someone's place during the World Cup, you have potentially hit the jackpot! However, there are pros and cons. Pros of staying with someone you know during the World Cup:

- Low or no cost! If you are lucky, this friend or family member may not charge you for your stay. If they do charge, it will be less than a hotel or Airbnb. If they don't charge, you should leave them a "little sum" as a token of appreciation.

- Local knowledge: Your host may know a lot about the city, show you around, and give recommendations and tips to maximize your experience.

- Staying with a local is the most authentic experience you can have. If you are lucky enough to have this option, embrace it.

- You can bond with your host and enjoy this shared experience, especially if your host is a World Cup fan. When I stayed with Faith in JoBurg for South Africa 2010, she was not a football fan. As a token of my appreciation for her hospitality, I took Faith to Durban for the Spain vs. Germany Semi-Final game. She had a blast on the trip, especially at the game. She is a huge football fan to this day.

- Staying with someone you know is convenient, just like staying at an Airbnb. You will have access to their entire home, including the living room, kitchen, laundry, etc.

Cons of staying with someone you know during the World Cup

- When staying with someone, there can be scheduling conflicts. There could also be differences in lifestyle and preferences. You may like nightlife and want to come home at 6 AM while your host gets ready for work or church.

- Your privacy is limited because you share a space with your host. It is their house, and they have their rules. Respect that.

- Expectation management: Be sure to set clear expectations. Yes, you know this person well, but can you share a living space with this person for two to four weeks?

Hostel. I have never used a hostel before. However, based on my research, it is a viable and cost-friendly option. Hostels provide a budget-friendly, social, and immersive World Cup travel experience. According to HostelWorld (2025), a hostel is a "Type of shared accommodation that helps your travel budget go further. But what you may not know is that the uniquely social nature of hostels will transform your trip." The following are the advantages of staying in a hostel during the World Cup:

- Hostels are very budget-friendly. They are cheaper than hotels and short-term rentals (Airbnb), making them perfect for the budget traveler.

- Hostels are very social due to shared spaces like kitchens and lounges. During the World Cup, you can meet like-minded people at a hostel.

- Hostels are usually located in city centers. Therefore, public transportation, stadiums, and fan zones are easily accessible.

- There are different types of hostels. You can choose a dorm, private, or shared room based on your preferences, comfort level, and budget.

Cons of staying in a hostel during the World Cup:

- Lack of privacy because you share a room with a stranger. Depending on the other guests, you may have to deal with varying noise levels, especially if a fellow guest's team wins a big match. It can get festive in the hostel during the World Cup.

- Depending on the hostel you choose, there are limited amenities. Do not expect a hotel vibe with daily room service, etc.

- You will share bathrooms and common areas, so be prepared for potential disruptions or inconveniences. For example, you may find the bathroom occupied when you need to use it.

- There are also security concerns when staying at a hostel. Depending on how the hostel is set up, you should keep an eye on your valuables and belongings.

Additional Tips and considerations for staying in a hostel:

- Hostels will be in high demand during the World Cup. Like hotels, Airbnb, and flights, you want to book as early as possible.

- Read hostel reviews from previous guests. Reach out to the operator. Are they responsive?

- Consider what amenities you need, such as a full kitchen, WiFi, or laundry facilities.

- Locations, location, location! You do not want to stay too far away from the action. If you stay far from the action for a lower cost, the money you save on lodging will be spent on transportation.

Two Teams and a Room

Russia 2018 was the first World Cup in which I stayed in a hotel. Being an Active Duty United States Air Force officer, and after all the security briefings I had to endure from Airmen trying to talk me out of going to Russia, I figured staying at a hotel would be best for me. I had checked out some Airbnb listings around Moscow, but I didn't see anything that grabbed my attention.

I found a Hilton hotel in Moscow for a reasonable nightly rate, so I booked it. It wasn't in the sexiest location in Moscow, a bit on the outskirts, but it would get the job done and give me a place to stay. My next step was to book my flight (with SkyMiles) now that I had finalized travel dates.

A few weeks later, Hilton emailed me saying a mistake had occurred when I booked my room. I was not supposed to have been able to book my stay at that hotel in Moscow because two World Cup teams had bought out the entire hotel. When I called to speak with a representative, I got an apology for the inconvenience. The agent told me that if I wanted to, I could cancel my reservation for a full refund and some Hilton Honors Points, or they could relocate me to the Hilton Moscow Leningradskaya. I would pay the rate for my original reservation. I jumped on the relocation offer that Hilton gave me.

I was upgraded from a 4-star hotel to Hilton's premier 5-star hotel in Moscow with no price change. Hilton Leningradskaya sounded familiar; I remember seeing it when I was searching for hotels in Moscow, and it was a quick pass due to the extremely high nightly rate. I hopped back on Hilton's website and checked out the details of the Leningradskaya Hotel, which was now "sold out." It was in central Moscow, with major train stations, restaurants, malls, and shops in its immediate vicinity.

While Joseph Stalin was in power, he built seven skyscrapers in Moscow. At the time, they were the tallest buildings in Europe (Express to Russia, 2025). The Hilton Leningradskaya Hotel is one of Stalin's "Seven Sisters" skyscrapers.

When I arrived at the hotel, metal detector machines were at the entrance. Every time I entered, I had to have whatever I was carrying go on the X-ray machine and walk through a detector, just like at airports. Why was there so much security? I wondered if this was how it was at hotels at all World Cups.

It wasn't too long until I found out why. I was staying in an official FIFA hotel. All the referees, linesmen, FIFA delegates, and leadership stayed at this hotel. Whenever I hit the gym at the hotel, there were always refs and linesmen/women working out on the treadmill. I also learned that when taking a picture with a World Cup referee, they won't take a photo with you wearing a football jersey. You have to take it off. That was interesting as I observed (from the hotel bar) while fans were taking pictures with Néstor Pitana, the referee for the 2018 World Cup final between France and Croatia (France won 4 - 2). This booking mistake led to my best free hotel room upgrade ever. Thanks, Hilton.

I hope I have helped you better understand the lodging options available at the World Cup and their advantages and disadvantages. I might consider staying in a hostel at a future World Cup for the experience. Don't make the same mistake I did by almost flying to the South Africa World Cup without any lodging arranged. The key is to book your lodging as early as possible to ensure peace of mind. The next chapter will examine what to expect when you leave your lodging to enjoy the excitement of the World Cup.

Navigating the Crowd

It is reported that about 1 million people visited Qatar during the 2022 tournament, and 0.3 million stayed in neighboring countries, using quick flights to get there (Bibolov, Miyajima, Rehman & Yuan, 2024). With so many people visiting one place in such a short time, it is quite an experience. This chapter will discuss the overall fan experience, fan safety, and Fan Zones/Festivals.

The Fan Experience and Culture

The fan culture and atmosphere at the World Cup are hard to explain. You have to experience it for yourself to truly understand. The World Cup officially focuses on the beautiful football game, but when you are at the World Cup, it is more than just a sporting event. It is a global celebration that brings millions of people to the same place to have a good time soaking up each other's infectious cultures, energy, colors, costumes, etc.

National pride is at its fullest at the World Cup. Presidents attend the World Cup to watch their teams play (President Bill Clinton was at my first World Cup game - Ghana vs. the USA). Fans wear their nation's colors, jerseys, flags, hair colors, etc. As I've mentioned before, my goal is to be in my seat for the national anthems. I do this to ensure I'm on time for the game, and most importantly, it's an incredible experience to be surrounded by people passionately singing their national anthems at the top of their lungs. The pre-game national anthems represent the ultimate moment when fans and players express their national pride and patriotism.

Fans at the World Cup are passionate! They cheer, sing, play drums, chant, and create vibrant atmospheres in stadiums, fan zones, restaurants, and the streets. Spontaneous eruptions of fans celebrating are common during the World Cup. I was watching a game in a restaurant during Qatar 2022, and there were four England fans at a table singing loudly and chanting the entire match; England wasn't even playing!

Learning about other cultures: With so many nations and cultures in the same place, you get to meet people and learn about their country and culture. This cultural exchange can be a cultural education through osmosis, where you are learning but don't even know it. This soaking in of other cultures and people allows us to return home with an open mind about people from different nations who love the game, good food, good drinks, and a good time just as much as you do. This experience also allows you to grow and be more open-minded about different people worldwide.

Festive atmosphere: The best of the host nation and host cities come out during the World Cup. There are street performers, stage shows, cultural events, live music, cultural food, you name it. As I walked the streets of Moscow in 2018, I was shocked at how many street rappers were rapping in Russian! Did you know Russia has its own trap music genre? I would have never known this had I not gone to Russia. When I was in Brazil in 2014, exploring Pelourinho, I would walk around a corner and bump into a cultural band in vibrant costumes, jamming on some snare and bass drums while marching and dancing down the cobblestone streets.

I attended the Ghana vs. Germany game in Castelão Stadium, Fortaleza, Brazil, in 2014. I might be biased, but this was the best and most entertaining game of the 2014 World Cup. Both teams were in all-out attack mode for the entire game. My seat for this game was in the middle of a massive section of German fans. They were singing and chanting before the game started, and they did not stop until the final whistle, when the game ended in a 2-2 tie.

It was contagious. Though I was there supporting Ghana, I could not help but return hugs and high-fives from the German fans when Germany scored. They showed love in return when I was the only person in the section jumping around when Ghana scored. The Ghanaian fans, especially those in the fanatic zone in the corner, beat drums and bounced on their feet for the entire game.

Unforgettable experiences

I have shared some of my unforgettable stories and experiences in this book; there are many more I haven't included for the sake of time. When you attend the World Cup, it will be an unforgettable experience. You will have stories you will find yourself sharing (or writing a book about) for the rest of your life.

These lifelong memories make you feel good when you go down memory lane and validate your decision to attend the World Cup. They say there are both good and bad sources of dopamine. Attending the World Cup triggers some of the highest forms of positive dopamine, which you will experience from traveling to a new place, achieving your goal of attending the World Cup, and social interactions with other fans (Benjo, 2023).

You could also make lifelong friends when you attend the World Cup. I have a few friends I only see at World Cups. We keep in touch via social media, and every four years, we meet for a drink and some food while watching a game at the World Cup. I plan to meet Miguel (the friend I met on my flight to South Africa in 2010) at the World Cup in 2026.

My good friend Juice is an Airman I served with and played football on our base team in Las Vegas. We hung out in São Paulo during the 2014 World Cup in Brazil and met again in Doha during the 2022 World Cup. Hopefully, we'll connect again during the 2026 World Cup.

You may be walking down the street and bump into an organized mob of fans from a specific country marching with flags, banners, a full band playing instruments, smoke bombs, flares, chants, songs, face paint, choreographed displays, etc. They are usually on their way to the stadium to watch their team play, celebrating a win, or just letting everyone know that their country is present at the World Cup!

Do your research, especially on the significant online football forums. You can find the national team support groups/bands/army (whatever they call themselves), where they will be watching games during the World Cup, what hotel they are staying, where they meet up before their team plays, what time they march to the stadium, and where they will be for their victory party. I was in one of these WhatsApp chat groups for the Team USA fan group in Salvador, Brazil, in 2014. I watched the USA vs. Portugal game with them in the middle of the main square in Pelourinho.

If you want to see how football unites the world, you must attend the World Cup. The fan experience is fantastic, and the amazing football games are just the cherry on top.

Safety First: Tips for Staying Safe in Large Crowds and Unfamiliar Environments

Safety is essential on any trip, including the World Cup. You should always abide by some essential and common-sense rules of traveling. Unless you are with a local or tour guide, don't go anywhere you have no business going. Respect the locals, laws, and culture. Do this, and you should be good in just about any country.

Before your trip: Get a good lay of the land. I pull up my hotel on Google Maps to see where it is in the city and what's in the vicinity. Familiarize yourself with the local laws and customs. For example, when in Qatar, a Muslim country, you must understand and abide by their laws, which are closely tied to their religion. Be sure to respect the laws and customs of the host nation.

Save the nation's emergency phone number in your phone. I also add an ICE number to my phone contacts. ICE stands for *in case of emergency*; this is a number first responders or hospital staff can call if something happens to you. It should be the phone number of your trusted emergency contact. Also, let that person know that you have them as your emergency contact so they'll know to answer the phone or call you back immediately if they miss your call.

It is also a good idea to save your home nation's consulate or embassy phone number just in case something happens and you need to contact them. Lastly, take a picture of your passport. Store it on your phone and in the cloud in case you lose your phone and passport.

I have never purchased travel insurance. However, it is a good thing to have in case you have a medical emergency, cancel your trip, or lose your luggage. I may consider this for the next World Cup. If something unplanned happens, I will want my family and me to be covered.

Inform your emergency contact (your ICE contact) or immediate family about your trip. They should know your travel dates, where you are staying, and how to contact you, your Airbnb host, or the hotel. It is always a good idea for someone to have a general idea of where you will be during the World Cup.

Before a trip, I call my cell phone carrier to check if their international plan works in the host nation and to learn more about their global plan. You can also get an eSIM for your smartphone during your trip. An eSIM, or embedded SIM, is a digital SIM card built into your smartphone that allows you to activate a cell plan without a physical SIM card. These are great for international travel. Some popular eSIM providers are Airalo, GigSky, Nomad, and Airhub.

During your trip: Stay aware of what is happening around you and look for potential threats. Keeping up with everything around you can be challenging at the World Cup as there is so much going on. Unfortunately, some crazy people take advantage of significant events to do bad things. Fortunately, the four World Cups I have attended have had no such incidents, and I hope this trend continues.

It is impossible to avoid large crowds at the World Cup. Just move with the flow of the crowd when you find yourself in one. If you ever feel overwhelmed by the crowds, take a break and find somewhere quiet to rest and recover before jumping back into the fun.

Regarding Personal Safety: Keep your valuables secure. It's the World Cup; you do not need to wear all your bling. This will only attract unwanted attention. Leave your valuables at home or in your hotel or Airbnb. It is still debatable whether you should always have your passport on you. I don't, so I suggest keeping a picture of your passport on your phone and in the cloud. Keep your phone and wallet secure, especially in large crowds where a pickpocket may lurk.

Stay hydrated! Rum and Coke alone won't do it. You must find time to drink water to keep your body functioning. Depending on the hemisphere, it can get hot or cold during the World Cup. World Cup 2010 in South Africa was winter, and temperatures were falling. The 2022 tournament in Qatar had to be moved to November and December since the heat would have been unbearable in June/July. Sunscreen, a hat, and glasses help protect you from the sun. You can spend all day outside during the World Cup at stadium games, doing touristy stuff, or at a Fan Fest. Be sure to stay hydrated and protected from the sun.

If you decide to drink alcohol, do not get sloppy drunk. Overindulging in alcohol makes you an easy target for robbers and thieves. In Qatar, public intoxication could get you up to six months in prison and a hefty fine. Try not to accept drinks from strangers. However, at the World Cup, this can be a tough rule to abide by; the atmosphere can become so festive. The drinks will be flowing if you hit it off with some incredible fans while hanging out, watching a game, or celebrating a big win. You have to trust your instincts. If something looks and feels funny, remove yourself from the situation.

Try to learn some basic phrases in the host nation's language. Also, have Google Translator on your phone. This app is extremely valuable and can get you through a communication barrier jam where nobody speaks the same language. Respect the local customs and people. Depending on your location, disrespecting locals can put you in danger. Even if it doesn't endanger you, it's simply not cool. Don't be that tourist. Another must-have app is WhatsApp. Even if you don't use it, download the app and get familiar with it. WhatsApp is how people worldwide communicate via text, phone, and video calls. All you need is a Wi-Fi connection to use WhatsApp.

Always keep a portable phone charger on you so your phone can charge while you enjoy the festivities. Also, put your phone on battery save mode as soon as possible to extend its use. I remember going to a few restaurants in Moscow that provided portable chargers free of charge. I was able to charge my phone while I ate.

Safety at the World Cup is paramount. I have not experienced any unsafe situations during the four World Cups I have attended. The worst I have seen were unruly, drunken fans. Overall, the World Cup is a safe event for all to enjoy. I was excited about going to Durban's Moses Mabhida Stadium for the Germany vs. Spain semi-final in South Africa 2010.

This stadium included a popular tourist attraction, the SkyCar. The SkyCar travels from the ground to a viewing deck directly above the middle of the stadium. I planned to check out the SkyCar, but for "safety and security reasons," FIFA shut down the SkyCar during the World Cup. FIFA takes security and fan safety very seriously at the World Cup.

Fan Zones and Festivals: Exploring Popular Fan Gathering Spots and Events

During my first World Cup, I had no idea that there were Fan Zones and Fan Festivals. I'm sure there was a Fan Fest in Joburg in an exotic location in Soweto, but I never went because I didn't know. When I was not at a game, I watched games where I was staying, restaurants, and bars. I didn't experience a Fan Festival until I went to Durban towards the end of my trip, and it was terrific.

FIFA organizes FIFA Fan Festivals. According to FIFA (2022), Fan Festivals are "temporary entertainment venues where fans could watch matches on giant screens and participate in a wide range of cultural and educational experiences free of charge." Fan Festivals require FIFA Fan IDs for entry. A Fan Zone is a viewing experience organized by the host nation. FIFA Fan IDs are not required to enter a Fan Zone. Fan Zones are a great place to be if you want to enjoy watching a game with locals.

As the experiences are similar, I will use the terms Fan Zone and Fan Fest interchangeably throughout this book. I have been to Fan Zones, which also had hosts on the main stage and live music, activities, food, and drinks. Everything you would enjoy at a FIFA Fan Fest happens at a Fan Zone. Even if you are not in the stadium watching the match, you can still have a blast at either one.

During Qatar 2022, the Fan Fests served beer. They were the only place in Qatar where alcohol could be consumed legally outside, a first for Qatar. I appreciate Qatar's cooperation with the world and its ability to allow beer at Fan Fests. I don't even enjoy drinking beer, but I had to take advantage of this rare, historic opportunity to chug a beer outside in Qatar while watching a match. I also respect Qatar's refusal to bow to international pressure and its prohibition of beer sales at the games. Their house, their rules!

Imagine attending an outdoor, all-day party or festival. Instead of your favorite band though, it's massive screens showing football matches all day and night. That's the best I can do to explain being in a fan zone or fan fest. If you don't have a ticket for the big game, the fan zone is an excellent option. These vibrant gatherings are for all fans. All flags, colors, songs, and chants in full display. You will witness expressions of joy unlike any other, with grown adults crying like babies in public. The World Cup brings out all levels of human emotions.

Massive screens, a massive sound system, bars, food—what else do you need? There is limited seating, so get there early or get creative when you arrive to make yourself comfortable. Fan zones are usually in very cool locations as well. I will never forget watching Uruguay vs. Holland while sitting Indian style in the sand at night on Durban Beach in South Africa with thousands of fans. That was amazing! I will never forget visiting the Fan Zone in St. Petersburg, Russia, to watch England vs. Colombia in the Round of 16 (1-1; England won in a penalty shootout). This fan zone was up against and under the Church of Spilled Blood. Have you ever seen a landmark while traveling and you take a picture every time you look at it? That's me and the Church of Spilled Blood. I could not stop looking at this architectural wonder.

It was much of the same at the Fan Fest in Moscow, with one of Stalin's massive skyscrapers looming behind the main screen in the background. Watching Brazil vs. Mexico at the Salvador, Brazil Fan Fest was memorable. I saw an online photo of the crowd that day from the lighthouse that overlooked the Salvador Fan Fest. I'm somewhere in that massive crowd!

Food! Did I mention there's lots of great food at the Fan Zones? Coca-Cola is always a major World Cup sponsor and has the beverages on lock. However, depending on the country, there may be some local food at the fan zone among all the usual food you would expect at a sporting event. Savor local and international flavors while you watch the game!

Fan Zones have music, DJs spinning tunes, musical performances, and a host on the main stage, giving away prizes and keeping the atmosphere festive pre-game, post-game, between games, and during halftime. Get your dance on, meet people, walk around, and check out the vendors, games, and activities. Not being in the stadium for every game doesn't even matter when you are at the World Cup. You can still have a great experience at a Fan Zone or Fan Fest.

At the World Cup, the fan experience is fantastic. It is even better to abide by some common-sense traveling safety precautions highlighted in this chapter. Now you know it is not the end of the World if you don't have a ticket to a big game. You can still have a blast watching the game with thousands of other fans in a Fan Zone or Fan Festival. The next chapter will cover what to expect when you do have a ticket for the big game.

The Match Day Experience

The big day has arrived. This chapter aims to convey what attending a World Cup match is like. I will also share my match-day routine that ensures I have everything I need to enjoy the pre-game, game, and post-game festivities.

Pre-Match Rituals: Sharing Pre-Match Traditions and Superstitions
It's game day, and you have a ticket! So, what do you do before the match? Depending on the time of the game, you can spend the day at the Fan Zone in the city where your match is happening or at a restaurant/bar watching games and ensuring you are well-fed before you head to the stadium. When game time approaches, head to the stadium. In Qatar, buses and the Metro were free for World Cup fans with a Fan ID. I would catch an Uber to the closest train station from my lodging.

In South Africa, Brazil, and Russia, fans had to figure out their way to the stadiums. Preferably, be in the city of the game the night before; however, being there the night before can be challenging due to little or no available accommodations. So, be within eyesight of the stadium at least two hours before kick-off. You win if you can find a restaurant or bar near the stadium. Never pass up the opportunity to eat, catch a game, and charge your phone before you head to the stadium.

My pre-match ritual is to have a good meal before I head to the stadium. I don't want to get hungry during the game and have to buy overpriced food at the stadium concession stand. I also don't want to risk missing a minute of the game waiting in line at the concession stand. Try to go to the bathroom before the game starts.

FIFA (2024) has a Stadium Code of Conduct that specifies items prohibited from the stadium and outlines acceptable fan behavior. Since the goal of this book is to help prepare you for attending a World Cup game, I must ensure you do not face rejection at the stadium gate due to a violation of the FIFA Stadium Code of Conduct.

Here are some highlights from the FIFA code of conduct: Do not bring any weapons or anything that could be used as a weapon to the stadium: no fireworks, sparklers, smoke bombs, or flares. Please do not bring pets to the stadium unless it is an assistance dog. No sports equipment, including footballs, are allowed. No outside food (this is why I always enjoy a hearty meal before heading to the stadium) and no drugs, narcotics, or stimulants.

Flags, flyers, clothing, or any political or offensive paraphernalia will get you stopped at the gate. The Code of Conduct for Qatar 2022 prohibited Vuvuzelas and any other device that produced excessively loud noise. Musical instruments are allowed into the stadium with written approval. This is how fan bands, brigades, and armies in the fanatic zone get their drums and instruments into the stadium.

No laser pointers, drones, or selfie sticks are permitted. If you have professional photography equipment, this is not the right time or place to bring it. You will be taking high-quality pictures of fans in the stadium parking lot because professional photography equipment is not allowed inside the stadium.

Regarding your behavior in the stadium, it's basic manners, home training, and treating others with dignity and respect. If you have always wanted a selfie with your favorite player, running onto the field to get that selfie is not the way to go. Regardless of how poorly your team plays, throwing objects onto the field is not allowed and could result in being ejected from the stadium and/or a visit to the local police station. This is why plastic bottles sold at the concession stands will be sold without caps. A full, capped bottle can be thrown quite far.

Be courteous to the fans around you, and try not to block the view of fans behind you. If your team is playing poorly, you may feel the need to motivate them with an assortment of expletives. However, excessive cursing is considered unacceptable fan behavior.

I know that may sound like a lot to keep up with. However, it's pretty simple if you are just a fan wanting to enjoy a game. To ensure I was good to go, all I brought to the stadium was my wallet, phone (my match tickets were on my phone), Fan ID, and portable phone charger (one power bank per person is allowed according to the FIFA Code of Conduct).

The Stadium Atmosphere: Describing the Excitement and Energy of a World Cup Match

Walking towards the stadium feels surreal. The stadium is lit up; you can hear the hum of excitement while helicopters and drones hover above. You can feel the energy in the air and the anticipation that you are about to experience something special. Also, be prepared to walk a lot. FIFA sets up perimeters around the stadiums. Cars are not allowed within a mile of the stadium. The best advice is to take public transportation or an Uber to get as close as possible to the stadium and walk the rest. FIFA has an outer and an inner perimeter around stadiums.

According to FIFA, "Where an outer perimeter is implemented, the majority of car parking facilities should be located outside this perimeter with the exception of dedicated and marked parking areas for players and officials, VVIPs, broadcast trucks, and equipment and emergency services" (FIFA Stadium Guidelines, 2024, para 27). If you can get close enough to the outer perimeter's edge, this is where you hop out of the car and start walking.

You will eventually reach the inner perimeter after walking with the crowd of excited, chanting, and singing fans. The inner perimeter is where you go through security and ticket checks. Once inside the inner perimeter, you have access to the stadium. Fans are always decked out in elaborate costumes and outfits for the game, representing their countries, even if their country is not playing in the game. These make for great photo opportunities. Take pictures with fellow fans and create lasting memories.

Qatar 2022 featured World Cup nations' themed traditional Arabic clothing, which allowed you to show respect for the culture while representing your team. I wore a Ghana-themed thobe and gutra to the Ghana vs. Uruguay match in Qatar 2022 (Ghana lost 2 - 0). During my walk to the stadium and to my seat, I was stopped every few steps by fans and families wanting to take pictures with me. It was all love, unity, fun, and respect.

Your ticket has a gate number, section, row, and seat. As my luck would have it, when I am running late, I always find out that my entry gate is on the opposite side of the stadium. This is why arriving early is best, just in case you need to walk around the entire stadium to reach your entry gate.

I always get excited as I approach my section because when I get to my section and walk through the tunnel, I see the field and the crowd for the first time. The field is so green, the stadium so massive, there are so many people in the stadium, and there is a lot of noise. After I snap out of this incredible feeling, I take a few pictures and videos and find my row and seat.

There is so much passion and energy in the stadium leading up to a game. The fans in the fanatic zone (in the corners close to the goals) are always already hopping, jumping, singing, chanting, and drumming. The Senegalese fans in Qatar 2022 got worldwide attention due to their energy and passion during their games. Their drums did not stop beating before, during, and long after the game.

I went to the Senegal vs. England match, where Senegal was eliminated (3 - 0). However, if you looked at Senegal's fanatic fan zone during that game, you could not tell they were losing the game. Their energy was contagious, and I'm sure it kept the Senegalese players motivated up to the final whistle.

The anticipation before the match is like nothing I have ever felt. The crowd erupts when the players walk out onto the field following the referees, and the lead referee takes the match ball off the display stand. The national anthems are played and sung passionately by a stadium full of patriotic fans and players. Then, the build-up to the first whistle ignites another phenomenal roar from the crowd.

When a goal is scored, the stadium erupts, and beer is spilled all over as people jump for joy (except for Qatar - no beer), hug, and high-five strangers; it is a roller coaster of emotions. Even as a neutral fan, you will feel the passion, and the deafening noise will make you smile and celebrate with your seat neighbors. It's a contagious passion. At the final whistle, you will never forget the experience.

One set of fans will be disappointed or in tears, completely saddened by defeat, and a few feet away, another set of fans will be in full victory mode, singing, chanting, waving flags, and ensuring the world knows their team won. Then, the neutral set of fans will be there, happy they experienced a great game and enjoy the post-match festivities.

Post-Match Celebrations: Recounting Post-Match Experiences, Including Victory Parades and Fan Gatherings

At the final whistle, you will never forget the experience. I've been to many games with amazing endings, high tension, passion, and unforgettable celebrations. I am trying to recall which was the best one, but there are too many. At the final in South Africa, watching Spain receive the World Cup Trophy and watching Iker Casillas, Spain's goalkeeper and captain, hoist the trophy to loud music, a light show, confetti, and a deafening roar from the crowd was exceptional.

I remember the heart-wrenching sadness at the Ghana vs. Uruguay quarterfinal game in South Africa in 2010. Ghana was about to be the first African team ever to make it to the World Cup semi-final. Luiz Suarez stopped what would have been Ghana's winning goal from crossing the goal line with his hand. Asamoah Gyan took and missed the penalty kick. The game went into extra time and Uruguay won the game. The entire continent of Africa was supporting Ghana. When the game ended, it seemed like every African in the stadium was crying. It hurt.

On a happier note, I attended the Ghana vs. South Korea game in Qatar in 2022 at the Education City Stadium. I don't want to sound biased, but this was one of the tournament's most entertaining games. The teams went at it for 90 minutes, playing total attacking football. For the last 15 minutes of the game, Ghana seemed to run out of gas. South Korea's attack was relentless. Ghana defended honorably, and South Korea could not find an equalizing goal. Ghana won the game 3-2, and the party was on! I attended this match with a friend from Ghana. I was fortunate enough to join a Ghanaian victory parade outside the stadium. The energy, joy, and passion were overwhelming!

We marched all over the stadium complex. The drumming, dancing, chanting, and singing did not stop! My friend knew where the official Ghana fans' hotel was, and that was the place to be that night. The hotel lobby hummed with passion, chanting, drumming, and singing. We went up to hotel rooms for drinks and authentic Ghanaian food. If you ever want to attend a grand victory party, hang out with the official Ghana fan club on the night of a big World Cup win. Later that night, we went to an African lounge and nightclub, Afro Wood Lounge Bar, in Doha, and the party continued into the early morning.

Speaking of nightclubs, if you are into nightlife, there is one last night to morning fan gathering. Every nightclub, lounge, or restaurant turns into club mode during the World Cup. This is how I met Oscar in South Africa. He worked at a restaurant/club in Joburg, and he couldn't believe I was there alone. He told me to come back to the club anytime I wanted. I took him up on his offer, and I was there almost every night I was in Joburg.

After the day's final match is played, the World Cup does not stop. The clubs are filled with fans wearing their nation's jerseys, waving flags, dancing, and celebrating (especially fans of winning teams). Every time Shakira's Waka Waka (This Time for Africa) or K'naan's Wavin' Flag was played, the club went crazy.

Brazil and Russia had much of the same energy at night. I remember going to a spectacular club in Moscow with a swimming pool in the middle of the club. Another nightclub in Moscow, Icon, featured a giant shark that would come down from the ceiling, bite a dancer, and lift her into the air high above the dance floor and clubgoers with her legs kicking and dangling.

Though it was a much more conservative country, I also enjoyed a few nightlife spots in Qatar. The African lounge, Afro Wood, stood out the most. This was where Africans living in Doha partied with visiting fans of the African countries in the World Cup.

Match day in the stadium can be a full-day experience. This is especially true if you pre-game with fans, your team wins, and you join the victory parade after the game and partake in the nightlife festivities into the next day. While this can be a long day, it is well worth it for the complete World Cup experience. After such an exciting day, you may want to relax a bit the following day and tour the host country.

Beyond the Pitch: Exploring the Host Country

The World Cup may be held in a city or country you've never visited, so make sure to carve out time for some sightseeing. This chapter offers ideas for activities on days without matches to watch or attend, enabling you to experience the host nation's culture fully. I have two regrets from my trip to South Africa: I didn't visit the Apartheid Museum in Johannesburg (I had no idea it existed until after I left), and I didn't go on a wildlife safari. Before your trip, research some of the major attractions in the host nation. You don't have to see them all, but it's good to know your options.

Cultural Immersion: Discovering the Host Country's Culture, History, and Traditions

Doing proper research before your trip can help you understand the country, its culture, and its laws. I'll be honest: Russia was never on my travel bucket list, and I am so glad I went to Russia when it hosted the 2018 World Cup. As I have learned from my previous travels, the media is powerful and will try to shape your perception of other countries and people for you.

Please don't fall for it. Do not let the media influence you and your travel decisions. Find out for yourself. Unfortunately, many of my usual World Cup buddies, whom I only see at World Cup events, did not go to Russia in 2018 simply because it was in Russia. They missed out on a fantastic travel experience and tournament.

With Qatar 2022, I can't believe how many people refused to attend because no beer was sold in the stadiums. If beer is why you didn't go to the World Cup, 1) You didn't want to go, and beer was a convenient excuse, and 2) You are not a true football fan. Folks who sat out the Qatar 2022 World Cup missed out on one of the best and most organized World Cup experiences. I was impressed by how the Qataris went above and beyond to ensure a top-notch fan experience. Qatar raised the bar in 2022. We shall see what the USA, Mexico, and Canada do in 2026 to maintain or exceed Qatar's high standard. The bar has been raised.

You can learn a lot about a country and its people during the World Cup. The Fan Zones often feature local food, music, dance, etc., things that show you the host nation's cultural identity. Walking around, you will pick up on many cultural cues and gems and learn how things are done in that country. For example, I had no idea there was rap music in Russia. There were rappers on street corners and in train stations all over Moscow spitting bars. Who knew!?

The media had painted such a poor picture of Russia in my head that I couldn't believe I was in Moscow. It looks like any other major city, with skyscrapers, restaurants, sidewalk cafes, people walking dogs, etc. While wandering around the Kremlin and Red Square, I saw the Changing of the Military Guards. It was a very cool ceremony to witness. I would not have seen it if I hadn't been exploring.

If you find yourself in Moscow, hungry, and searching for a spectacular view, visit Ruski Ice Bar. This restaurant, located on the 84th floor, boasts a room entirely furnished with ice-made items. Café Pushkin's food was so nice that I had to eat there twice. Don't let biased people and the media talk you out of making lifelong, priceless memories. See and find out for yourself.

In Qatar, I immersed myself in the Souqs, where you can spend hours shopping, eating, and people-watching. I also got custom suits made at a Souq Waqif in Doha. Whenever I travel to another country, I try to seek out and eat at a Jamaican restaurant. I discovered One Love Restaurant in Doha, and the food hit the spot! I also visited Qatar's national museum and learned much about this small nation's history. I spent about four hours in that museum.

I also spent a day at Katara Cultural Village in Doha. I sat on a bench, people-watching and enjoying the water and skyline view. Suddenly, the Qatari military marching band appeared and marched past me, complete with rifles, drums, and bagpipes. The sound of the bagpipes in this military marching band revived memories of the band at my alma mater, The Citadel. Katara had it all: restaurants, boats, boat rides, shops, art, museums, and a mosque, which I toured.

I also took a three-day trip to Dubai to do some touristy stuff there. I deployed to the United Arab Emirates in 2006. At that time, it looked as if the entire city of Dubai was being constructed all at once. I needed to return to see the outcome of all that construction. I was impressed.

In Brazil, I was excited about my extended stay in Salvador, Brazil. It is where slave ships brought stolen Africans to Brazil. Therefore, there is a strong African influence and culture. I wanted to experience it, so I visited the Afro Brasileiro Museum in Salvador. I learned that Brazil had more enslaved Africans than any other nation during the trans-Atlantic Slave Trade. I also learned that even today, Brazil has the highest population of black people outside of Africa. It was the same horrific slavery story that I was used to in the USA and the Caribbean, just in a different language (Portuguese).

While walking around Salvador, locals would talk to me in Portuguese. I blended in, and that was a fantastic feeling. That was until I opened my mouth, and they would be surprised, laugh, and call me "gringo," their affectionate term for a foreigner.

I also got to see Capoeira live for the first time while wandering around and exploring Pelo. Enslaved Africans developed this Afro-Brazilian martial art style and integrated acrobatics, dance, drums, songs, and rhythm (Capoeira Arts Center, 2025). I grew up watching movies and playing video games that featured capoeira.

I also got to experience Sao Paolo, Rio de Janeiro, Natal, and Fortaleza, Brazil. Unlike my previous trips to Brazil, where I only experienced Rio, the World Cup had me moving all over Brazil to see games and experience different parts of the country's culture and history.

In South Africa, I walked around Soweto Johannesburg and people-watched. In Cape Town, I took the cable car to the top of Table Mountain to enjoy spectacular views of the city and the ocean below. I also took a trip to Cape Point, the southernmost point of the African continent.

I took the ferry to Robben Island, where South African heroes and freedom fighters like Nelson Mandela were imprisoned. An interesting part of the Robben Island experience is that the tour guides were former political prisoners there. As expected, this tour left me with a heavy heart, but I had to experience it.

When I traveled to Durban for the Spain vs. Germany semi-final match, I had no idea what a cultural experience awaited me. I was unaware I would fly into King Shaka International Airport, which made my day! Growing up in Jamaica, I watched the Shaka Zulu TV series and absorbed every minute of every episode. Years later, I bought and rewatched the DVD box set many times as an adult. I also read his biography, *Shaka: The Story of a Zulu King*, and was fully immersed in that book from beginning to end.

Unfortunately, the original King Shaka statue at the airport was removed during my visit. The new King Shaka statue was unveiled in November 2024. I'll have to return to see it. While exploring Durban, I witnessed Zulu performers in traditional warrior clothing singing and dancing to traditional Zulu songs. I didn't realize I would be in the heart of what was once the Zulu empire, where the Zulu tribe still holds significant influence in South Africa.

You never know what childhood memories, heroes, and lifelong idols might resurface while exploring the host nation at the World Cup. I know it can be hard to get away from the football games, but do yourself a favor and devote at least one day to being a tourist.

If the city you are in offers one, purchase a ticket for a hop-on, hop-off double-decker tour bus. Make the entire loop and take note of all the stops. On the second loop of the tour bus route, get off the bus at the most interesting stops and explore. You may never get back on the bus. Exploring on foot may lead you to other stops along the tour bus route. Open your mind and fully immerse yourself in learning about the host country's sights, culture, and customs.

On a red double-decker tour bus in Moscow, I met a female fan from the USA. We both expressed how amazing our time in Moscow had been. She said she didn't understand the big deal the US government and media made about Russia. We were both impressed and glad to be there enjoying the World Cup.

One of the coolest parts of doing touristy stuff during the World Cup is that you'll be touring with other fans. This means that while you're immersed in the host nation's culture, you may learn about other cultures as you make friends with other fans on the tours. It's incredible how much you can learn when everyone you talk to is from a different country!

Take advantage of free activities while you enjoy your World Cup trip. Museums may have free admission on some days. Look up free walking tours of your city (be sure to tip the tour guide). There are also parks in most major cities with free events. If all else fails, take a walk - you never know what hidden gems you will discover. This is especially true during the World Cup.

When traveling internationally, always use the local currency. When you use your debit/credit card, always go with the local currency if you are asked what currency you want to pay in. Using the local currency for a debit or credit card gives you a better exchange rate. If possible, use a credit or debit card that doesn't charge foreign transaction fees.

I never step foot outside the airport in another country without some local currency in my pocket. Yes, I know the currency exchange rates at airports are horrible. However, for peace of mind, I prefer to have some local cash in my pocket to get me through my first twenty-four hours. The better option is to find an ATM in the airport and get your cash there. ATMs usually offer the best exchange rates, and they are hassle-free.

Do your research about tipping. Is this a tipping country? Or will people look at you like you are crazy when you try to tip them? If it is a tipping country, this is another excellent reason always to have some local currency in your pocket. Find out how much (in the local currency) makes a decent tip, and keep those bills ready for when you get some excellent service.

Make sure your payment methods are compatible with the host nation. In South Africa in 2010, I was asked about "a chip" when I went to restaurants and tried to pay with my debit card. I had no idea what the servers were asking me about. The server would talk to the manager, and they would eventually take my debit card payment. I started carrying more South African rand on me just in case my debit card was rejected.

It wasn't until 2015 that chip-enabled credit and debit cards were rolled out mainstream in the USA. When my bank sent my new chip-enabled debit card, I said, "Ooohhh! So, this is what they were asking me for five years ago in South Africa!" I appreciated that South Africa was not messing around with debit/credit card security.

Local Cuisine: Exploring Local Delicacies and Culinary Experiences

Food is one of the best things about traveling to other countries. Please do not be afraid to venture beyond stadium food and explore local markets and street food vendors. Nothing beats a hot, fully loaded chicken shawarma from a street vendor after a night of partying!

After the Ghana vs. South Korea game in Qatar, I visited the hotel where the official Ghana fan group stayed. Delicious traditional Ghanaian food was prepared and served to everyone there to enjoy. For my cocktail enthusiasts, I had a Moscow Mule in Moscow. I had a White Russian in Russia. I had a Black Russian in Russia.

When I was in South Africa, I ate zebra. I didn't even know zebra was food! If you are ever in Cape Town, check out Mama Africa. It's a great restaurant. Be sure to visit the local restaurants, especially if you are staying in a hotel. The hotel restaurant may be super convenient, but you may not get an authentic dining experience representative of the country.

I followed a rule while in the military and traveling internationally for work. US chain restaurants were off-limits, and we only dined in local establishments. I applied this rule during World Cup trips to ensure new culinary and cultural experiences.

I broke this rule in Sao Paolo, Brazil, when I ate at Fogo de Chao, only because this location was unique; it was the original Fogo de Chao restaurant location. I love Brazilian churrascarias, and while in Brazil, I made it my mission to enjoy as many of them as possible. If you enjoy getting the "meat sweats" and trying to keep up with the servers continuously bringing you skewers loaded with meat, you'd have had a culinary enlightenment in Brazil in 2014.

I deployed to Doha for work in 2012. While there, I fell in love with a restaurant, Kebab King. When I returned to Doha for the World Cup, it was on! There is something about those Kebab King platters loaded with meats, nan, and hummus. There's something extra special about lamb chops in Middle Eastern countries. I can eat them all day on a platter with nan and hummus.

Food tours are another great alternative. These can be found via Airbnb Experiences or through your hotel concierge. If you talk to a local, ask them for recommendations. Where locals eat and where tourists eat can have completely different vibes and experiences.

After spending many hours sitting in an aluminum tube five miles above the Earth to be in the host country, you might as well go all in, be adventurous, and explore the culture. When trying local foods, clearly express your dietary restrictions using Google Translate. Step out of your culinary comfort zone and embrace the local culture, landmarks, and cuisine while at the World Cup. You won't regret it.

The World Cup Community

I don't know if World Cup fever is real, but I do know that during the World Cup, there's a sense of love and unity among people from all over the world. Everyone is happy, approachable, and helpful—not just the tourists and fans but also the locals. This chapter will explore the sense of community and positive energy I have felt and experienced at the World Cup.

Meeting Fellow Fans: Sharing Stories of Connecting with Fans from Around the World

One of the things that makes the World Cup a special event is the connection you can make with fans from around the world. As Kamau (2024) put it, "For fans, it is not just about the matches; it is about the memories, connections, and emotions that make the tournament truly special" (para. 21). I could not agree more. It is a special feeling that one must experience to understand truly.

I met people in South Africa in 2010 and I am still in touch with them. One was my buddy Oscar, who worked at a sports bar that became my nightlife spot when I was in Johannesburg. Oscar and I connected, and he gave me the lay of the land in Jo-Burg—and man, did we party. Oscar moved back to

Zimbabwe, where he is from, and had a son. His son's first name is Prosper, and he is my godson. I'm going to see Oscar again and meet Prosper one day.

I met a couple of guys in South Africa in 2010. We kept in touch and reconnected in Brazil in 2014. We picked up where we left off as if we'd seen each other daily during the four-year gap. One went to a university in Boston, where my ex-girlfriend (still a friend) went. I asked if he knew her, and he did! Imagine being in South Africa, calling your ex-girlfriend in the USA while hanging out with one of her college friends. Attending the World Cup puts you in a position to create priceless moments and connections.

I attended the Iran vs. Bosnia and Herzegovina game in Brazil in 2014 at the Fonte Nova Arena in Salvador (Bosnia won 3 - 1). I was not expecting the Iranian team to take to the field with the Lil John and East Side Boyz song, "Turn Down for What!" Iran was ready to play. I struck up a conversation with a couple sitting next to me. It turns out they were from New Mexico, USA. I told them I have a co-worker from New Mexico who's always bragging about her homemade green chile. When I told them where I worked, it turned out that they knew my co-worker. Are you serious!?!?

From Wakanda to Russia!

After I watched Russia eliminate Spain at the Fan Zone in Red Square, Moscow, the entire city was in the streets celebrating and chanting RUSSI-A! RUSSI-A! RUSSI-A! It was wild! It seemed like the whole city was in the streets. People were on top of cars, climbing light poles, and waving Russian flags.

Walking through a sea of festive Russians, I entered a restaurant with many TV screens where fans watched the Croatia vs. Denmark game. This restaurant was packed, with large tables where groups could sit. I approached a group with an open seat at a table and asked/gestured if I could sit there. They gestured that the seat was free, and I sat down.

A lady in the group tried to talk to me, but it did not work out well since I didn't know Russian, and she knew very little English. So, we opted for Google Translator for some small talk. The usual stuff: Where are you from? What's your name? Am I enjoying Russia? The phone was being passed around the table for the Q&A session between the group and me as we got to know each other. Here, I learned that the younger generation in Russia has no beef with the USA. They shared that they were born after communism ended in Russia and knew very little about it.

When the phone returned to the lady who initiated the conversation, she spoke Russian into it for Google Translator to work its magic, and she handed me my phone. It read, "Are you from Wakanda?" The smash hit movie Black Panther hit theaters a few months earlier, in February 2018. Who knew Russians were watching Black Panther?

I didn't say a word. I looked at her and gave her a crisp, sharp Wakanda salute. Her eyes lit up, and she responded with the Wakanda Salute. We all laughed and high-fived, and the entire table joined in and gave me the Wakanda Salute. They ordered my drinks for the rest of the night while we enjoyed the game and each other's company.

I have noticed in my solo travels that when I tell locals I am traveling alone, they go out of their way to ensure I have a good time. They take extra time to give me recommendations and ask if I need anything. It is a beautiful thing when this happens.

A Happy Hour to Remember

I met two beautiful sisters in a restaurant and lounge, Cubana, in Cape Town, South Africa, in 2010. They refused to believe I had traveled from the USA to South Africa alone and were confident I could not have done something so bold. When they were finally convinced, I told them about my journey from Las Vegas and how I ended up in Cubana that night. They said they had to keep in touch to ensure I was OK while I was in Cape Town. They also made sure I knew all the best places to visit in their city.

I was in Cape Town because there was no way I would be in South Africa and not tour Robben Island. Unfortunately, tickets were sold out earlier that day. I got tickets for a future date. I flew back to my base in Joburg for a few days, then returned to Cape Town for the Robben Island Tour.

I was in touch with the Mzansi sisters via text while on Robben Island. One of the sisters told me, "Paul, enough of this touristy stuff. When you get back to Cape Town, we are going to take you to The District." I didn't know what The District meant, but it sounded like a great plan! When I got off the Robben Island Ferry in Cape Town, the sisters waited for me in the parking lot. I hopped in the back seat, buckled up, and we were off to The District.

I saw the Cape Town skyline getting smaller and smaller in the rearview mirror as we drove for about 30 minutes on the highway. We exited the highway and made a few turns. It became apparent to me that "The District" is the hood! When we parked, I saw stray dogs, small, neat rows of houses, and jovial, friendly people moving about, doing their daily business. It reminded me of Kingston, Jamaica, where I was born. I took a nice deep breath and inhaled all the splendor of returning to what felt like familiar territory. I followed the sisters into a building that had no sign.

When I entered this building, it looked like a butcher shop. There was a U-shaped glass counter and lots of different meat under the glass. One of the sisters handed me a large aluminum bowl. She asked me, "What do you want to eat?" while gesturing at all the meat on display. I pointed out the meats I wanted, and an employee behind the counter piled them into my bowl.

I followed the sisters through another door when my bowl was piled high. This area was dark, hot, and smoky. Wood fires burned, and cooks without shirts worked their culinary magic. The sisters stopped me before a spice rack and told me to pick the spices I wanted. I picked a few, and they told me to give the spices and my ten-pound bowl filled with meat to the cook.

Next, we walked through one final door, and we were in a club, sports bar, lounge, and restaurant with TV screens all over. A World Cup game was on the main projector screen. A DJ was spinning afro beats and afro house music while people vibed to the rhythm on the dance floor. I glanced at my watch; it wasn't even 5 PM yet! The older sister turned to me and said, "This is how we do happy hour in The District."

We found a table, ordered drinks, and enjoyed the vibe. About 15 minutes later, a server brought a bowl loaded with deliciously cooked meats and a half-loaf of sliced white bread. There was no knife and fork at this party; we reached into the bowl with our hands and enjoyed this meal together.

I had so many memorable moments in South Africa 2010: my first World Cup, my first World Cup game ever, attending the infamous Ghana vs. Uruguay game, seeing Nelson Mandela in person for the first time on the field before the Final a few days after seeing his former prison cell on Robben Island, attending the Final, and seeing Spain lift the trophy. But this happy hour is my favorite moment of South Africa 2010. It was so simple, so unplanned, and so perfect.

You may write a book about your World Cup experiences one day. Journaling your thoughts and feelings about the World Cup as you experience them can help enrich your memories and your book as you read the details of your journey 20 years later. Your long flight home is the perfect time and place to jot down your thoughts and experiences.

The Global Football Family: Discussing the Sense of Unity and Camaraderie Among Football Fans

The unity and camaraderie among football fans is unlike any other. From my experiences, conversations, and observations at the World Cup, I realized that many of the world's problems are caused by governments, not by the people. It is all love at the World Cup. Fans help fans, socialize with fans, and make lifelong friends with fans regardless of race, sexual orientation, gender, religion, etc.

The Beautiful Game and the Baggage Caper

I scored tickets for the USA vs. Ghana game at the Arena das Dunas in Natal, Brazil. I flew to Natal from Sao Paulo for the game and then to Salvador afterward. Natal had built a new airport for the World Cup, the Greater Natal International Airport. A lot of us on the flight were going to the game. However, there was a problem. Most of us had luggage, and there was no way we could take it with us into the stadium.

There were a good number of US fans on this flight. We asked the flight attendants if the new airport had storage lockers. There weren't any. We were in a bind and had to figure out what to do with our luggage so we could enjoy the game, which started a few hours after landing in Natal. Two or three fans on the flight said they had rental cars. We devised a plan to load up the rental cars with all our luggage, find somewhere safe to park the cars, and then go to the stadium to enjoy the game.

There I was, in Natal, Brazil, for the first time, in a taxi packed with my new friends from the flight, following three rental cars stuffed with our luggage to a parking spot in a shopping center reasonably close to the stadium. We had about four taxis following the three rental vehicles. After the game (USA won 2-1), we reconvened in the shopping center parking lot.

There was a popular Brazilian churrascaria where we parked the cars. We were hungry after spending the last two hours in the stadium. We walked to the restaurant, had a great meal, talked about the game, and got to know each other. Then, we returned to the airport with all our luggage intact, ready for our next World Cup adventure.

The Impact of the World Cup: Examining the Social and Economic Impact of the Tournament

The World Cup is a major event with far-reaching impact. The tourism boost it brings to the host nation(s) is incredible, bringing billions of dollars to the host nation. I can only imagine how much business hotels, restaurants, and the transport industry get during the tournament. Bibolov et al. (2022) shared that the World Cup in Qatar boosted the tourism economy in neighboring countries.

The World Cup causes host nations to create new or improve existing infrastructure. For example, the newly built airport in Natal, Brazil, was built for the World Cup. Now, the people of Natal enjoy a modern, state-of-the-art airport. Host nations also invest in new stadiums used after the World Cup by local teams and to host local events. New hotels and other buildings are constructed for the World Cup, and these infrastructure improvements have a long-lasting positive impact on the host nation.

Job creation: Qatar hired thousands of workers from other nations during the World Cup. They were posted everywhere, equipped with megaphones, inside train stations, outside stadiums, and along busy routes. They ensured fans easily got to Fan Zones, stadiums, and train stations; it was impossible not to know how to get to the Metro in Doha during the World Cup. Qatar also donated 3,000 buses, stadiums, and stadium seats to Lebanon (Gulf News, 2022). Not only does the World Cup promote amazing fan love and camaraderie, but this happens among nations, too!

The World Cup is a huge platform that can be used to raise awareness of various social issues, such as human rights, racism, poverty, discrimination, and environmental protection. I like that FIFA uses its platform to raise awareness of these social issues. Acknowledging that these problems exist is the first step to solving them.

Qatar hosted the first World Cup in the Middle East. The first major issue was when to hold the tournament. The schedule changed because Qatar would have been too hot in June and July, so this World Cup was held in November and December. Most of the major domestic football leagues worldwide had to pause for a month due to the World Cup.

Alcohol in a Muslim country also came under the spotlight. I am glad Qatar stood firm against international pressure to allow beer in the stadiums. Their country, their rules. I saw the pictures of warehouses stacked to the ceiling with pallets of

Budweiser not being shipped to stadiums. People decided not to go to the World Cup over beer. However, Budweiser, a major World Cup sponsor, got a small win, and those beer pallets were allowed to be consumed in the FIFA Fan Festivals.

Homosexuality is illegal in Qatar, with a possible three-year prison sentence (CNN.com, 2022). FIFA and many domestic leagues worldwide show their support for the LGBTQ community by players wearing rainbow armbands. Additionally, fans in the LGTB community were not going to the World Cup and publicly called out Qatar about the illegality of homosexuality in the country.

According to the Qatari government, "Everyone is welcome in Qatar, but we are a conservative country, and any public display of affection, regardless of orientation, is frowned upon. We simply ask for people to respect our culture" (CNN.com, 2022). This sounded like a reasonable request to me.

The World Cup is the ultimate experience for fan connections and camaraderie between strangers from around the world. It is proof that the world can come together every four years and enjoy a month-long tournament, and it's mostly all love between the fans and locals. The impact the World Cup has on the world is immense. I guess that is what I was feeling in 1986 as I watched the World Cup for the first time. I knew it was something special I needed to experience for myself.

Lasting Memories

Some of the best memories of my life are from attending four World Cups. Once you attend one World Cup, you must go to the next one. That first experience hooked me, and I keep returning to the World Cup every four years to make fresh, lifelong memories.

Reflecting on the Journey: Summarizing Key Takeaways and Lessons Learned

Going to the World Cup gives you time to reflect. Your long trip home is the perfect opportunity to reflect on your experiences at the World Cup. During my LAX layover after my flight from Moscow to Los Angeles in 2018, I posted the following as my closing thoughts for my World Cup 2018 photo album on Facebook:

"I'm still reflecting on my first trip to Russia and here's what I have so far (Yes, I am aware of issues at the government levels. This is my reflection as a tourist mingling with the common people):

Biggest takeaways: Don't believe the hype! Go see for yourself. I remember all the side-eyes and strange looks I was getting when I told people I am going to Russia for the World Cup... simply based off what they heard somewhere. Book the flight and go! The media is VERY powerful!

The same thing happened with World Cup in South Africa 2010, if I could have easily let what I read and watched on TV about South Africa keep me home. It simply wasn't true...there was nothing but love in South Africa! The same for Brazil 2014 with health scares and "stadiums won't be ready" propaganda...none of this doom and gloom was a factor!

If all the language was removed from the street signs and you were dropped off in the middle of Moscow, you would not be able to tell what major world city you were in. Burger King, McDonald's and KFCs everywhere (I even saw a Krispy Kreme!), people are walking to work, walking dogs, rollerblading, curbside cafes, parks and people doing what we do all over the world. The unanimous agreement between myself and just about every foreigner I met in Russia was, "What's the big deal? This place is just like anywhere else, the food, vibes and people were very helpful & awesome!" Was it World Cup fever? Maybe, but the locals in Russia were adamant that that's how it is there every day.

The younger Gen-X and millennials did not grow up in communism and they said maybe some older Russians may have a problem with folks from the USA and foreigners. Overall, super-dope trip! I'm going back. I also need to hit up Armenia, Uzbekistan...hell...all the "stans"!!! & Colombia!!?? OOOWWEEEE!!! yeah...on top of the future travels list! Well done FIFA & Russia...arguably the best World Cup ever! BIG-UP yuhself France!

Who's rolling with me to Qatar 2022?"

The World Cup Legacy: Discussing the Enduring Impact of the World Cup on Personal and Global Levels

The World Cup impacts so many people on a personal and global level. It unites passions from all over the globe, and attending a World Cup is an emotional rollercoaster. I still feel pain when I think about how Gyan missed a penalty kick for Ghana against Uruguay in 2010. I will never forget watching so many Ghanaian fans cry in the stadium.

I will never forget the joy of Landon Donovon's last-second winning goal against Algeria. I watched Russia eliminate Spain in Red Square, Moscow, with Russians and saw Moscow go nuts into the wee hours of the morning. Moments like this are why you go to the World Cup.

Each World Cup inspires future generations of football players. I remember watching my first World Cup in 1986. When my brothers and I played football in our yard in Jamaica, I became Careca or Josimar, two Brazilian legends. My brothers were Maradona and John Barnes. We were inspired, and we hadn't even attended a World Cup. I can imagine what taking your children to a World Cup can do. It is one of my goals to take my son (11 months old) to a World Cup game one day.

On a global level, the World Cup is a rocket ship for the host nation's economy. Bringing together so many cultures in one place exposes people to intercultural understanding and tolerance of other cultures. I firmly believe that traveling the world makes you more intelligent than someone who has not traveled outside their country.

The World Cup is the ultimate excuse to get out and visit another country. While mingling with people worldwide you subconsciously learn to have an open mind and embrace cultural differences. While enjoying the World Cup, you subconsciously increase your cultural capital.

Just as people better understand each other's cultures, the same applies to diplomacy and diplomatic significance between nations. Presidents and Prime Ministers attend the World Cup and have opportunities to hold informal meetings with other heads of state that can build positive relationships.

According to Smith (2018), the four most politically charged World Cup Games ever were:

Italy vs. France, 1938—This was one year before World War II started, and Italy was a fascist nation then. It is reported that Mussolini told the team to "win or die." Fortunately, the Italians won this game.

East Germany vs. West Germany, 1974—Germany was split into two nations after World War II. One side represented communism, and the other represented democracy. East Germany won this game, but West Germany won this World Cup.

Argentina vs. England, 1986—This match was four years after Argentina's and England's Falklands War. Argentina got some payback and won this game. England may have won the War, but Argentina won the 1986 World Cup.

United States vs. Iran, 1998—Political tensions between the USA and Iran have brooded for around 50 years. The US Embassy hostage crises in Iran and the Iranian Revolution are some key events behind the high tension between these two teams. Iran won and knocked the USA out of the tournament.

Speaking of the United States, President Donald Trump has started a trade war with Canada and Mexico via tariffs. He is also sharing his desire for the USA to annex Canada to become the 51st US state. President Trump has escalated the US and Mexican border tensions with aggressive immigration policies and rhetoric. Mexico's President and Canada's Prime Minister have not taken these threats, tariffs, and policies lightly. President Trump has named himself the Chairman of the USA's 2026 World Cup Task Force (Associated Press, 2025). Will these political tensions impact how these three countries jointly host the 2026 World Cup?

Smith (2018) shared, "While it may not always be the case, major sporting events do have the capacity to improve relations between nations in conflict" (para. 19). I sure hope he was right. The World Cup does bring fans together despite political tensions. Football brings the world together.

Planning for the Future: Encouraging Readers to Plan for Future World Cup Adventures
BOOK YOUR TRIP & GO!

I'm not just saying this to say it. I did it despite the hurdles and challenges I faced in 2014.

The House, The Flight, and The Opening Match

In April 2014, I moved from Oklahoma to Colorado. Since I had already booked my flight to São Paulo, Brazil, for the World Cup opening game between Brazil and Croatia, I only had a month and a half to find and purchase a house in Colorado before leaving for Brazil. I spent the month exploring houses all over Colorado Springs until I found one that truly appealed to me. I made an offer and negotiated with the seller about a few details, and they ultimately accepted my offer. When my realtor informed me of the closing date, I was shocked. The closing date was two days after my scheduled flight to Brazil.

What would you do? Cancel your trip? Reschedule your flight to a later date after the closing? Or just go to the World Cup?

I was staying in a hotel then, and the costs were increasing. Through the network of Jamaicans in the U.S. Air Force, I connected with a fellow Airman named Donovan in Colorado Springs. When he found out how long I had been living in a hotel, he offered me a place to stay at his home while I continued my house hunt. This was a tremendous relief and eased the financial strain of paying for a hotel and eating out three times a day. I shared my closing date dilemma with

Donovan and asked if he would represent me at the closing if I arranged for a Power of Attorney. He kindly agreed!

I flew to Brazil as planned to enjoy the World Cup. Being in São Paulo during the opening game, watching alongside thousands of Brazilians at a public gathering, was an unforgettable experience (Brazil won 3-1). I returned home a few weeks later, and Donovan handed me the keys to my brand-new house.

I could have used my housing situation as an excuse, but I continued my trip and went! At that time, I had a Brazilian visa, so I didn't need to purchase a match ticket in advance to enter Brazil. While in Brazil, I attended several games using the third-party methods mentioned in Chapter 2 of this book. I booked my trip and went!

Just Go!

Stop making excuses, end the analysis paralysis, get off the fence, and attend your first World Cup. The experience will stay with you forever. I smile and feel good whenever I have World Cup memories; it is the ultimate dopamine hit. If you don't attend the next World Cup, you only compound the FOMO (fear of missing out). Get that FOMO monkey off your back and attend an upcoming World Cup.

In this book, I aimed to outline the unbelievable levels of belonging and human camaraderie that only happen at the World Cup. It is hard to explain, but you feel and experience it at the World Cup. I shared some stories that best convey the connections, memories, and sense of adventure of attending a World Cup.

I also wanted to share the key areas of consideration when planning to attend a World Cup. You are good to go as long as you have a place to stay and documents to enter the host nation legally. So what if you only have a ticket for one game? Go and figure out the rest when you get there. You can get tickets to games and/or enjoy the positive vibes of Fan Zones when you get there. Just go!

If you plan early, you can find budget-friendly flights and lodging options for your World Cup trip. You may even know people who live in the host nation, which could reduce a significant expense. Flying and lodging using loyalty reward points are tried-and-true strategies for traveling to the World Cup without destroying your budget.

From my experience, the World Cup is one of the safest events on the planet. Of the four World Cups I have attended,

I have never experienced a security scare. Book your trip and enjoy the World Cup with peace of mind!

Book your trip, grab your passport, create your World Cup adventure, and make new friendships that will last for the rest of your life. Secure game tickets and book accommodations as soon as possible. Stay safe and healthy. Capture and make lasting memories. Most importantly, have fun!

I look forward to us bumping into each other in 2026 in the USA, Canada, or Mexico.

Thank You!

I want to thank you for purchasing my book. There are so many books out there, but you chose to purchase and read mine, and I appreciate it.

I have a small favor to ask. Would you mind posting a review on the platform? As an independent author, I can use all the support possible, and leaving a quick review would mean a lot to me.

Your feedback would go a long way toward helping me write more books that will help you achieve the results you desire.

Thank you in advance for your review and support.
https://amazon.com/review/create-review/?&asin=B0DWPN88F2

References

Associated Press. (2025). President Trump to lead 2026 World Cup Task Force. Espn.com. https://www.espn.com/soccer/story/_/id/44155171/president-donald-trump-task-force-2026-world-cup

Benjo. (20203). Good & Bad Sources of Dopamine. Medium. https://benjo-li.medium.com/good-bad-sources-of-dopamine-d75492afc8d9

Bibolov, A., Miyajima, K., Rehman, S., Yuan, T. (2024). 2022 FIFA World Cup: Economic Impact on Qatar and Regional Spillovers. International Monetary Fund. https://doi.org/10.5089/9798400267864.018

Capoeira Arts Center. (2025). Capoeira History. ABDA-Capoeira Arts Center. https://www.abada.org/capoeira-history/#:~:text=Capoeira%20(pronounced%20ka%2Dpoo%2D,for%20more%20than%2040%20years.

Choy, M., Salbu, R. (2011). Jet Lag; Current and Potential Therapies. *Pharmacy and Therapeutics*. NIH.gov.

https://pmc.ncbi.nlm.nih.gov/articles/PMC3086113/#:~:text=Jet%20lag%2C%20also%20known%20as,travel%20across%20multiple%20time%20zones.

CNN. (2022). "It's not safe and it's not right." Qatar says all are welcome to the World Cup but some LGBTQ soccer fans are staying away. CNN.com. https://www.cnn.com/2022/11/19/football/qatar-world-cup-2022-lgbtq-rights-spt-intl/index.html

Cultural Understanding; FIFA Fan Festivals and Fan Zones. (2022). Publications.FIFA.com. https://publications.fifa.com/en/final-sustainability-report/social-pillar/cultural-understanding/fifa-fan-festival-and-fan-zones/

Express to Russia. (2025). Stalin's Seven Sisters Skyscrapers in Moscow. Expresstorussia.com. https://www.expresstorussia.com/guide/stalin-s-seven-sisters-skyscrapers-in-moscow.html

Federation Internationale de Football Association (FIFA). (2024). Stadium Code of Conduct. FIFA.com. https://www.fifa.com/en/search?q=stadium+code+of+conduct

Federation Internationale de Football Association (FIFA). (2024). Stadium Guidelines 5.1: Precinct and Perimeter. https://inside.fifa.com/technical/stadium-guidelines/technical-guidelines/stadiums-guidelines/precinct-and-perimeter

Federation Internationale de Football Association (FIFA). (2022). Disabled Fans offered unique FIFA World Cup experience. Inside FIFA. https://inside.fifa.com/social-impact/news/disabled-fans-offered-unique-fifa-world-cup-experience

Fragomen. (2022). Qatar: Relaxed Requirements for 2022 FIFA World Cup Visas. Fragomen.com. https://www.fragomen.com/insights/qatar-relaxed-requirements-for-2022-fifa-world-cup-visas.html

Gulf News. (2022). Qatar to donate World Cup Buses to Lebanon. Gulf News.

https://gulfnews.com/world/gulf/qatar/qatar-to-donate-world-cup-buses-to-lebanon-1.92877090

Hostelworld Blog. (2025). What Is a Hostel? The Answer Will Change Your Travels Forever. Hostelworld.com. https://www.hostelworld.com/blog/what-is-a-hostel/

Kamau, M. (2024). How Fans Around the World Celebrate the FIFA World Cup. Cleats. https://vocal.media/cleats/how-fans-around-the-world-celebrate-the-fifa-world-cup-z7wnh074d

Motson, J., Brownlee, N. (2006). Motson's World Cup Extravaganza. ISBN: 1-86105-936-1

Smith, Rob. (2018). Here are 4 of the most politically charged World Cup games ever played. World Economic Forum. https://www.weforum.org/stories/2018/06/here-are-4-of-the-most-politically-charged-world-cup-games-ever-played-russia2018/

The World Cup Guide. (2024). Buying Tickets to the World Cup. theworldcupguide.com.

https://www.theworldcupguide.com/buying-worldcup-tickets/

www.ingramcontent.com/pod-product-compliance
Lightning Source LLC
Chambersburg PA
CBHW021203130626
46554CB00005B/1966